A Spiritual Handbook

A Resource for Travelers and Guides on the Journey

James Galluzzo

Gray Wings Press, LLC
Milwaukie, Oregon
2011

A Spiritual Handbook
A Resource for Travelers and Guides on the Journey

By James Galluzzo

Library of Congress Control Number: 2012940676

ISBN 978-0615629995

Acknowledgments

Exercises and Meditations
By Peg Edera

Reflections on the Spiritual Journey
By James Michael Whitty

Responses to Reflection Questions
By fellow travelers and guides

The book is modeled after the Urban Spirituality Spiritual Direction
Training program: EMBRACING THE HOLY.

Special thanks to the dream team that helped create this program:
Tracy Stone, Elaine Joseph, Peg Edera, Ruth Nickodemus
and James Galluzzo

To a fellow traveler: Sr. Pat McCrann

And to the two teachers in the program:
Peg Edera and James Galluzzo

Thanks to those who helped edit this book:
Jan Kruger, Susan Hammond, Annie Doyle, Janet Beard, Andrew Morrow,
Kathy Fanning, Gerry Grover, and Ruba Byrd

Cover Design by Karen Gatens, Gatens Design

VI.

Chapters

A Spiritual Guide for a Spiritual Journey
James Galluzzo

This is a handbook for those going on a spiritual journey and for those who are guides and mentors for travelers on the journey. A reflection or meditation exercise follows each chapter to offer a better understanding of the material. Quotations are provided at the end of each section as prompts for reflection, conversation, or journaling. The questions are offered to inspire a writing practice to allow each person to get a clearer picture of how the topic relates to his or her spiritual journey. Travelers and guides offer their responses to each of the questions.

"The longest journey begins with a single step." Lao-tzu

Spiritual Journey

I'm goin' on a spiritual journey, saving up my fare.
With nickels, dimes, and dollars worth of lessons to get me there.
Sail oceans of unknowing, hike hills of jagged stone;
Shake with wild abandon when that last train whistles me home.

Goin' on a spiritual journey, I'll leave that list behind.
No matter what I crossed off, it got longer all the time.
Just like the endless desert, all sun and desperate wind,
And nothing there was moving but the sweat upon my skin.

This morning I picked up a stone to prove that I had lived.
Walked it 'round the dog park, dropped it from the bridge.
And I hope that stone is happy at the bottom of that stream
Where ripples shift the sunlight and the world is sparkling clean.

But who knows how we end up where we do…

Goin' on a spiritual journey, Lord knows I'm traveling light:
A tattered bag for dreams, a prayer for insight.
Cuz when I pray, "Thy will be done," that's all there is to say.
On the twisting Road to Find-out, only forgiveness knows the way.
Only forgiveness knows the way.

© Joe Uveges (from the CD *When Freedom Calls*)
used with permission

Introduction

I have been on a spiritual journey for 50 years of my life. After going to a spiritual guide for 25 years, assisting others with spiritual direction programs, being a mentor and spiritual guide for over 20 years, I decided it is time to share my experiences of the journey as both the traveler and the guide.

I want to hold out a model for a spiritual journey. The model is for anyone willing to go on the journey, willing to ask the hard questions and willing to sit with the messy and the wonderful. It is for those who are in transition, who are longing to move, who are ready for transformation in life. It is also for anyone who wants to be a guide, mentor, or ally to those on a spiritual path.

To set the stage for this book, spirituality is defined as the connection to one's self, others, the world/universe, and to whatever is transcendental in life: the Divine, God, energy, Source, Being, the universal questions.

When a person decides to look at his or her spirituality (that inherent spiritual quality that is in each person) there are three areas that are essential in order to have a rich experience on the journey: creating a safe space, being present, and listening.

This book will focus on the journey from each person's personal stories and lived experiences. It begins where each person is at the present moment.

Others talk about spirituality in a much narrower sense, pointing out that it is concerned with matters of the spirit, a concept closely tied to religious belief and faith. Spiritual issues are those matters regarding humankind's ultimate nature and meaning, not only as biological organisms, but as beings with a relationship to that which is perceived to be beyond the senses, time, and the material world. The problem with this narrow view of spirituality is that it sets up a dichotomy between spirit and body.

Still others talk about spirituality as if it only encounters a God, Spirit, or some form of the Divine. Spirituality is seen as how God or the Divine comes into one's life, how the Divine wants a person to live, and what the Divine wants one to do in life situations. The problem with this view is that it puts God above the human person and separates—rather than allows for—a relationship based on mutuality.

This book will focus on the model of the spiritual journey that is based on "telling one's story." This book defines spirituality as part of all that a person is, the core of one's being, the heart, soul, mind, and body. It is living life out of full humanity.

-- James Galluzzo

Definitions

Spirituality is the connection to self, others, our work in the world, the earth, the universe, and whatever is transcendental in each person's life.

Guide is a person who is on a spiritual journey of his or her own and walks with a person who is beginning the journey or wanting to travel deeper on the journey. Others may use the term **spiritual director**.

Traveler is a person wanting to explore her or his spirituality and who interviews guides to walk with him or her on the journey. Others may use the term **directee**.

Chapter One

Spiritual Journey

The spiritual journey begins when a person starts to ask questions about these things:

- life, the meaning of being human
- the place of suffering in the world
- the role of peace and justice
- the stuck places
- what brings fear
- what brings hope
- how the Divine fits into the story
- where the movement is taking the person
- where the holy is

As these questions stir, the traveler begins to sit with the questions and look for another traveler who is asking the same questions or for a guide who has been on the journey. It begins with the pursuit of the spiritual journey and with the search for a guide who can direct or guide the traveler in the pursuit of the questions or new insights. It is important to have a guide, because as a traveler looks into the questions, all kinds of stirrings take place. These stirrings can cause any number of feelings such as anxiety, hope, curiosity, or discernment. The stirrings can bring up questions about where a person is, what the person is doing, and what challenges make him or her rethink some of the basic principles that have guided the traveler's life up until the discernment started. But the traveler needs to remember that through the questioning and stirring—through the messiness, the uncertainty, and the confusion—there will be movement that will bring liberation and transformation.

For the traveler, the journey begins when the person gets in touch with the questions that are stirring. This means the traveler must take time to be quiet, to listen, to begin the search, and to look for a guide to help on his or her journey.

For the guide, the journey begins with doing his or her own work, asking his or her own questions, being faithful to the spiritual practices, having a guide, continuing spiritual education, and having a supervisor to help with work of being a guide.

The journey is an ongoing adventure; the traveler never finishes pursuing the truth on the journey of life. It is essential that the traveler chooses a guide to walk with along the way, because the quest is filled with new adventures, challenges, and emotional baggage. It is important for the traveler to choose the right person. Travelers should always interview two or three guides and then listen to the inner voice, intuition, or what the heart is saying. Pick a guide who feels right, who listens well, and who is present to what is being asked.

The spiritual journey is about questioning, stirring, and movement. It is not about getting to a destination. Life is filled with possibilities and with new thoughts, ideas, ways of thinking, ways of practicing, and ways of living.

It is never boring; it is always rich with excitement and opportunities to fulfill dreams.

Quotations on the Spiritual Journey

While Lao Tzu may have said: "The journey of a thousand miles begins with one step," in today's Internet age, your own journey of a thousand websites begins with one click, and this is it, this is it, this is it! ❧Deepak Singh

Pilgrims are poets who create by taking journeys. ❧ Richard R. Niebuhr

The longest journey is the journey inwards of him who has chosen his destiny. ❧ Dag Hammarskjöld

The world is a traveler's inn. ❧ Afghan saying

You cannot travel the path until you have become the path. ❧ Gautama Buddha

Do not seek to follow in the footsteps of the men of old; seek what they sought. ❧ Matsuo Basho

To stay in one place and watch the seasons come and go is tantamount to constant travel: One is traveling with the earth. ❧Marguerite Youcenar

Stripped of all its outer encrustations, spirituality emerges as a science, as scientific as any other, as verifiable in its results. Let any seeker take it up and let him create in the laboratory of the soul the conditions that are prerequisite; as sure as the day follows the night shall he rise into the Kingdom of God. ❧ Sant Kirpal Singh

Questions on the Spiritual Journey

1. Which quotation on the spiritual journey most speaks to you?

2. What are you longing for?

3. Think about creating a safe place, being present, and listening. Which of the three concepts is most mysterious to you at this time? Why?

4. *"Out beyond ideas of wrongdoing and rightdoing, there is a field. I'll meet you there." –Rumi (tr. C. Barks)* Have you ever been there? What does this quotation say to you?

5. How does being fully human fit into your idea of spirituality?

6. What in this school called life is the lesson you have spent the most time on? What is the lesson for now? What is one of the lessons you are looking forward to addressing?

Response to Questions on the Spiritual Journey

1. Which quotation on the spiritual journey most speaks to you?

"The journey of a thousand miles begins with one step," speaks loudly to me. I always felt I had to have the whole trip planned before I could begin. How freeing this quotation is for me.

2. What are you longing for?

I am longing for my life to be less hectic and less about other people's needs. I am longing for peace, quiet, less anxiousness, and less struggle between service and self-care.

3. Think about creating a safe space, being present, and listening. Which of the three concepts is most mysterious to you at this time? Why?

Creating a safe space is the most difficult for me. I spent most of my life not feeling safe. I have all kinds of reasons for not feeling safe based on real experiences, real fear, and imagined fear. It has been long in coming to understand the concept of safe space, and it was through nature that I found a space that allowed me to feel safe, happy, and at peace.

4. *"Out beyond ideas of wrongdoing and rightdoing, there is a field. I'll meet you there." –Rumi (tr. C. Barks)* Have you ever been there? What does this quotation say to you?

Through traveling with my spiritual guide I have been able to feel that I am embraced for who I am and whatever I bring to the table. It is an amazing experience to be in the field or back in the garden where life is good, where questions are honored, and where it is all right to be "in the messy" and face my demons.

5. How does being fully human fit into your idea of spirituality?

Until I found a space of safety, I never really looked at my own humanity. It is in the safety of nature and the safety of my guide and my true friends that I feel it is OK to embrace my humanity, my story, my gifts, my struggles, and my hopes.

6. What in this school called life is the lesson you have spent the most time on? What is the lesson for now? What is one of the lessons you are looking forward to addressing?

I have spent most time on seeing myself as good and enough. The lesson for now is to live my life believing I am good, loved, loving, and loveable. It might be time to look at where I want to be in retirement and how am I going to let myself be loved as I back away from taking care of people.

Chapter Two

Spiritual Direction: The Work of the Traveler and Guide

The term *spiritual direction* is often misunderstood. It does not refer to directing another person's journey. Other language is often used, for instance, allies, spiritual mentors, soul mates. This book refers to the roles as *traveler* and *guide*, meaning the same as *directee* and *director*. No matter what terms are used, it is important to understand where the history and tradition of spiritual direction comes from and to realize that most of the resources and literature use the term *spiritual direction*.

The guide's work is the practice of sitting with the traveler as he or she attempts to deepen the relationship with the sacred or to learn and grow in his or her own personal spirituality. The person who seeks direction shares stories of his or her relationship with self, others, the world, the work in the world, and whatever is sacred to the person. It deals with how he or she is experiencing spiritual issues. The guide creates a safe place, listens, and asks questions, and then is present to assist the directee in his or her process of reflection and growth. Spiritual direction develops a deeper relationship with the spiritual aspect of being human. It is not counseling; it is about supporting a person on her or his journey.

The guide and traveler's work can take place in an individual retreat setting, a group retreat, or a one-to-one setting. During the daily retreat meetings, exercises—or spiritual disciplines—are given to the directee as a way to continue his or her spiritual growth.

Regular direction involves a one-hour meeting every four to eight weeks, which offers more ongoing time outside of retreat direction.

In Christianity, spiritual direction has its roots in the early Church. The Gospels describe Jesus serving as a mentor to his disciples.

The *Spiritual Exercises of Ignatius of Loyola* is a guideline for spiritual direction during a retreat or one-on-one session.

In Judaism, the Hebrew term for spiritual guide differs among traditional communities. The verb *hashpa'ah* is common in some communities, though not all; the spiritual guide called a *mashpi'a* occurs in the Habad-Lubavitch community and also in the Jewish Renewal community.

Spiritual mentorship is customary in the Hasidic world.

The guide and traveler continue the tradition of spiritual direction, which has been a part of the spiritual journey for many years.

Quotations on Spiritual Direction

Spiritual direction is, in reality, nothing more than a way of leading us to see and obey the real Director—the Holy Spirit hidden in the depths of our soul. ❧ Thomas Merton

Christian spiritual direction is the process of accompanying people on a spiritual journey. Spiritual direction exists in a context that emphasizes growing closer to God or the sacred, the holy or a higher power. Spiritual direction explores a deeper relationship with the spiritual aspect of being human. Spiritual direction is helping people tell their sacred stories every day. ❧ Spiritual Direction International

The object of spiritual direction is to cultivate one's ability to discern God's presence in one's life—to notice and appreciate moments of holiness, to maintain an awareness of the interconnectedness of all things. ❧ Rabbi Jacob Staub, Jewish

Islam means to surrender to God in peace. The journey of surrender is the lifelong work of transforming the ego, opening the heart, and becoming conscious of God. We need to bring the Divine into the center of our lives. The guidance, inspiration, and support of a guide are crucial to this process. ❧ Jamal Rahman, Muslim

Spiritual direction is the contemplative practice of accompanying a person or group as they waken to the spiritual in everyday life. ❧ Dale Rhodes, Taoist

Spiritual direction is the contemplative practice of helping another person or group to awaken to the mystery called God in all of life, and to respond to that discovery in a growing relationship of freedom and commitment. ❧ James Keegan, Jesuit

Spiritual direction is a time-honored term for a conversation, ordinarily between two persons, in which one person consults another, more spiritually experienced person about the ways in which God may be touching her or his life, directly or indirectly. In our postmodern age, many people dislike the term "spiritual direction" because it sounds like one person giving directions, or orders, to another. What we call it doesn't make any difference. The reality remains. It is conversations about life in the light of faith. ❧ Unknown

Questions on Spiritual Direction

1. Which quotation on spiritual direction most speaks to you?

2. What role has spiritual direction or working with a guide played in your spiritual journey?

3. What is it like for you to be the traveler, or directee?

4. What is it like for you to be the guide, or director?

5. How has the process of spiritual direction affected your role as guide?

Response to Questions on Spiritual Direction

1. Which quotation on Spiritual direction most speaks to you?

The quotation about accompanying the traveler on the spiritual journey in everyday life most speaks to me. It is easy to look at spiritual questions on a retreat or during time off, but to live it daily is challenging to me.

2. What role has spiritual direction or working with a guide played in your spiritual journey?

I would not be where I am without a spiritual guide over the past several years. With the guide's presence I have done lots of healing work, have had many opportunities to discharge old hurts, have broken open my life story in many creative ways, have been listened to in ways I have never experienced before, and have built a deep relationship of trust, honesty, and holiness.

3. What is it like for you to be the traveler, or directee?

It is humbling, freeing, amazing, challenging, hard work, worthwhile, and the richest experience in my life.

4. What is it like for you to be the guide, or director?

It is a wonderful opportunity and a gift to listen to one's story, to travel with someone, to be present to another human being, and to experience the mutuality of walking with someone else who is on their journey.

5. How has the process of spiritual direction affected your role as guide?

I no longer need to fix the other person, take on their issues, or be responsible to other people. I have learned to be present to whatever the person brings to a session, to help the traveler take responsibility for their work and their journey, and listen without taking on other's burdens. I have learned about graced moments and a deep understanding of mutuality.

Chapter Three

The Three Most Essential Elements

for a Spiritual Journey

Every journey has some requirements—like a passport, ticket, boarding pass, or foreign currency. The spiritual journey has three elements that are essential for the journey to take place. It is impossible to go on the journey without these three essential elements.

The three elements are *creating a safe space*, *being present*, and *listening*. The journey will not get off the ground if any of the three are missing. These elements are necessary for both the person on the journey and for the guide.

The first element that is necessary is that there is a safe space for the traveler and the guide to share, listen, be silent, and hear the spirit or energy that will point the direction. Without safety the sharing will be limited, the truth held back, and the guide will not have the necessary pieces of the traveler's story to offer the best direction or support.

The next element required is to be present. If the traveler is not present to what is unfolding, then he or she will be lost and will not remain on the path. Being present allows the traveler to stay connected to what is taking place in present time and keeps the person from being stuck in the past or fretting or longing for the future. The guide must be present if he or she is going to support the direction that is unfolding in present time. If the guide is not present then the traveler will feel lost or abandoned and trust will not be established.

A traveler cannot go on the journey if he or she does not listen to the inner voice that tells the traveler it is time, what questions are stirring, where to begin, and what direction to take. Listening is essential before the traveler can even begin. The guide must be a good listener if he or she is going to support the traveler on the journey. If the guide isn't listening, then the traveler could end up wandering alone, without an advocate.

Quotations on the Three Key Areas

Listening is a magnetic and strange thing, a creative force. The friends who listen to us are the ones we move toward. When we are listened to, it creates us, makes us unfold and expand. ❧ Anonymous

Only the present moment exists. Time is an illusion, and the past exists only as a memory stored in the mind, while the future is imagined, a projection of the mind. ❧ Eckhart Tolle

However far modern science and techniques have fallen short of their inherent possibilities, they have taught [human]kind at least one lesson: nothing is impossible when we are safe to tell the truth. ❧ Anonymous

Chapter Four

Creating a Safe Space

For a traveler to explore a spiritual journey, it is essential that he or she have a safe space in which to share his or her story. This becomes a major role of the guide. The guide creates or helps the traveler create a refuge, a space providing safety, shelter, protection, aid, and relief. The story has many wonderful memories, challenges, and struggles. Creating a safe space, being present and listening sets the environment for a traveler to begin to build trust. How often is a traveler given good attention? How often is the traveler truly listened to? How often does he or she have a guide who is there no matter what he or she has to say?

Emotions play a big part in the traveler's story and sometimes even prevent her or him from sharing certain pieces of the story. Emotions often get in the way of safety. Emotions can tend to dominate actions and decisions. Emotions are often mistaken as signs of weakness. This causes the feeling to be shoved inside, and then the focus is put on what the feelings are instead of clear thinking. But no matter how much one wants to avoid the feelings or bury the feelings, it is important to be reminded that everyone is a human being—and that every human feels, acts, thinks, and decides. A safe space is necessary for the traveler and guide to use all his or her human functions. Feelings are simply feelings; some are good and some are hard to take, but remember, feelings are all just feelings.

On the spiritual journey, the traveler encounters all kinds of feelings, both positive and negative. Regarding the negative, if the traveler can develop a trusting relationship, then he or she can begin to discharge the feelings of unhealed hurts and pains. Remember, the traveler would have dealt with the negative experience when it happened if there had been a guide available to listen and be present when the hurt happened.

There will also be positive experiences on the journey.

The traveler does not try to bury the feelings of joy, peace, or serenity. He or she takes the feelings in and learns from the feelings. That is what a spiritual guide can help the traveler do with the challenging feelings of fear, anger, resentment, or pain. The guide can help the traveler deal with the feelings, face them, feel them, and let go of them. This can take place only if there is a safe space for this action to happen.

The guide and traveler can create a safe space by choosing a special room or a spot in nature. Or the guide can set up a small altar, or can set a candle or another symbol that relates to the traveler's story or has meaning for the journey. It is not so much the space, as it is making the environment safe and welcoming for the traveler.

When the safe space has been established, then the process can begin. For example, suppose there is a situation where a disagreement with someone takes place, and it affects the rest of the day. The day can be filled with regret, anger, resentment, and distraction. Experiencing this, the traveler will go home in an even worse mood. On the way from work, he or she won't be able to see the sun shining, or might be tempted to stop at the grocery store and buy a favorite comfort food. All this could take place because a negative thought had the power to contaminate the way the traveler perceives the reality around him or her.

When this happens, if the person has a safe space to relax the mind, it will do wonders for the traveler. It can be an actual location or an imaginary space. If there is a problem on the mind and it just won't go away, the traveler can go to that safe space, that personal sanctuary. It can offer a relief; it can allow the traveler to just sit with the feeling or to discharge the feeling. The best idea is to totally immerse one's self in the space where one can feel the anger and resentment. If the traveler doesn't have a safe space or place to go to, that is not a problem; just create an imaginary space or ask the guide to help you find a space. In that safe space, the traveler faces the feelings, feels them, and discharges them. Then the traveler can reconnect to him- or herself, think well, and imagine new ways of being, thinking, and living free of distress. The mind moves from the negative thoughts and starts processing a whole new way of being.

A safe space can be found in any number of forms. It can be a song, a memory, a place in nature or with a friend. While in the safe space, the primary thing is to let the traveler become completely involved in whatever is "up" for him or her. Once the traveler has faced and felt whatever has come up, then he or she can reconnect to his or her true self. He or she may still get flashes of the problem or negative feelings every now and then, but the feelings will have less power because the traveler has faced the negative, felt it, and let go of the power of the feeling.

This is a vital stage in the solution to what is bothering the traveler. He or she will come back from the "safe space" with an increased energy level. The traveler will feel better about him- or herself and obtain more confidence about removing any obstacle or settling any issue. This is how a small refuge from a harsh reality can increase the traveler's healing energy and free a traveler or guide to solve even the most difficult problems.

Again, the guide can play a large part in helping the traveler create a safe space or in creating a safe space for the traveler to become welcomed into.

Meditation on Creating a Safe Space
by Peg Edera

A refuge is a place of rest and healing. It is a place in which change can begin. It is a place you can return to again and again for comfort, care, and solace. It is a place in which you can remember who you uniquely are, where you can call yourself home to yourself and collect the pieces that may have gone astray.

One of the privileges of being a spiritual director (guide) is offering refuge. We offer it in the *temenos* or scared space we create when we meet our directees (travelers). We offer it in our promise of confidentiality. We offer it in the respect and love we hold as central principles of our call. Never underestimate the transformative possibilities of refuge.

In this meditation you return to a place of refuge you remember, or you can create one anew.

Begin by finding a quiet, warm, and comfortable corner. Sit on the ground or a cushion or in a chair with your feet on the ground.

Let stillness settle over you like a soft blanket, and let your eyes close.

Feel your breath all through your body. For three or four breaths, inhale deeply and exhale slowly and completely.

With your mind's eye, your imagination, go to a place of refuge. If you remember a place, recall it in every detail: the colors, the textures, the smells, the sounds, even the taste in your mouth. If you cannot recall a place of refuge, imagine one now. Imagine all the details.

Stay here for as long as you desire.

Before you leave, reflect on these questions:

> What do you see around you? What is the air like?
> What makes this place a refuge?
> What does this place offer you?
> How does your body feel in this place?
> What part of yourself can you claim here?
> What part of yourself can you remember here?

Before you leave your refuge, place your right hand over your heart, say thank you, and remind yourself that this place of refuge is always available. Make a promise to return soon.

When you are ready, softly and slowly open your eyes and return to this time and this place.

Quotations on Creating a Safe Space

Last night I dreamed that I was sleeping. And in this sleep, I dreamed that I was in a safe space. ❧ James Galluzzo

A soul mate is someone who has locks that fit our keys and keys to fit our locks. When we feel safe enough to open the locks, our truest self steps out and we can be completely and honestly who we are; we can be loved for who we are and not for whom we're pretending to be. Each unveils the best part of the other. No matter what else goes wrong around us, with that one person we're safe in our own paradise. Our soul mate is someone who shares our deepest longings, our sense of direction. When we're two balloons, and together our direction is up, chances are we've found the right person. Our soul mate is the one who makes life come to life. ❧ Richard Bach

The ache for home lives in all of us, the safe space where we can go as we are and not be questioned. ❧ Maya Angelou

I want some space to heal, some space I can laugh and cry and just "be," no judgment—just love. ❧ Unknown

Questions on Creating a Safe Space

1. Which quotation on creating a safe space most speaks to you?

2. Where is a place in nature that you love to visit that feeds you?

3. Where is a safe place where you choose to go to be quiet?

4. How do you create a safe place for yourself in the middle of your busy daily life?

5. As a guide, what are ways you can create a safe space for the travelers who come to you?

Response to Questions on Creating a Safe Space

1. Which quotation on creating a safe space most speaks to you?

"The ache for home lives in all of us, the safe space where we can go as we are and not be questioned," is my favorite quotation on safety. When I found a guide, I finally experienced safety.

2. Where is a space in nature that you love to visit that feeds you?

I used to go walk a beach that was close to the house when I was in Florida. It was quiet; I felt alone with nature. Now there is a path close to home I go to and walk. The path is smooth and flat with trees, bridges, creeks and wildflowers. Sometimes when I walk it, I call my sons or a friend in Florida. Other times, I walk the path and admire the wonders of nature. I have watched a pair of raccoons play on the bank of the creek and stepped over a small snake crossing the path. On the other side of the trees are homes and a golf course. I enjoy the quiet, calming feeling I get. There are benches along the way; however, they are in the sun at the time I walk past. At one end of the trail, there is a park and baseball field. If there is a game going on, I usually watch the children for a while before turning back. My family spent many years at the baseball park when we were growing up. At the other end of the trail is a playground and picnic area. Although I have never sat down and rested, this is a place one could rest, relax, and read a book under the trees.

3. Where is a safe space where you choose to go to be quiet?

I go to the living room when I want to be quiet. I will light some candles and sit in the couch when I want to meditate, or I will sit in "my chair" with my feet on the hassock when I want to sit quietly and reflect on the day. I will usually light the candles in the fireplace and on the different tables. There is a lighted rock garden on the coffee table that I like to light. I do not turn on the lamps. Depending on my mood, I will sometimes turn on soft music.

4. How do you create a safe space for yourself in the middle of your busy daily life?

During the work week, I am generally working alone in my cubicle. However, I do go outside for walks on occasion. Sometimes, with a co-worker, we walk around the parking lot two times in the am and pm. Although it is not a daily habit right now, I still will go out for a walk—or when it is raining, I zigzag the stairs for six floors when I need to get away.

5. As a guide, what are ways you can create a safe space for the travelers who come to you?

It would be a quiet place without distractions; a comfortable place so they would be able to relax. I would light a candle and offer a cup of tea or glass of water to drink. We would sit facing each other for eye connection. I would want a feeling or atmosphere of trust and safety.

Chapter Five

Being Present

The gifts of the Magi were gold, frankincense, and myrrh. The gift today is the gift of presence. The traveler on a spiritual journey needs to be present to his or her story and to the questions, stirrings, and movements that take place. The guide has to be present to what the traveler is sharing through his or her words, feelings, and body language. The traveler and guide will be companions, present to each other.

Presence is a noun, not a verb; it is a state of being, not a state of doing. Being is not highly valued in a culture that places a high priority on doing. Yet, presence or "being with" another person carries with it a power—to bear witness to a moment, to listen to a traveler's story or journey, to help carry an emotional burden or to begin a healing process. In it, there is a human connection with another. Presence is also defined as the "sacrament of the moment," being at communion with the present.

Often a guide does not know what to say or do when a traveler's story is heard or his or her pain or struggle is shared. The guide doesn't have to say anything or do anything. It is often enough to just be there, to be present.

When a guide learns to be present, he or she does not hesitate to be in the presence of others for whom he or she could "do" nothing. One can sit at the hospital, be with a friend, sit with someone in a coma, and be with someone who is dying. Each present experience is a journey of a traveler's life. Sometimes when a person comes out of a coma, the person says there was someone there who was present.

The guide might be pulled by the need to *do* more than *be*. Yet, repeatedly experiencing the healing power of connection, a bond is created by being fully there, by being present to another. Where the guide is present, the traveler is never truly alone.

The power of presence is not a one-way street, not just something the guide is to the traveler. As the traveler experiences the power of presence, it helps the traveler to be present to others in his or her life. Presence is always mutual and always empowering.

Being present is a challenging concept, and it is central to the spiritual journey of any traveler or guide, in any tradition. It is a necessity for both the traveler and the guide.

The direct experience of the present for each human is that it is what the power of "now" is here. Direct experience of the present is true for all humans, because all human beings are connected. For all, "here" means "where one is" and "now" means "when one is." Thus, the common experience is that the present is inherently linked to the traveler, to his or her story, to where the traveler is on the journey.

From the perspective of time, the concept of "now" is a tiny point on a continuous timeline that separates past from future. It is not clear, however, that there is a universal timeline—or whether, as relativity seems to indicate, the timeline is inherently linked to the observer or the story teller or traveler.

The timeline view of "now" may not hold the full picture, but the qualities of "now" or the "present" in the human direct experience are very different from the qualities of past and future, which are available only through memory or anticipation. In the human direct experience, "now" has a certain aliveness, reality, and immediacy that is not part of the experience of past and future. Indeed, any experience is always happening "now," even in the living of some past event. Thus, there is a deep philosophical case for saying that the present moment is all there ever is, from moment to moment.

The past contains history; the future contains hopes, and the present is where the traveler and guide are.

Some even go so far as to say that each present moment holds eternity.

Meditation on Being Present
by Peg Edera

The Practice of Being Present

Begin by considering a situation or a dilemma that has caused or is causing you concern. Review the details.

Now bring your focus to the meeting place of your mind. Let your mind take charge. Working with just this meeting place, consider: What is your best thinking on this? What strategies could you employ here? What is your goal?

Now, shift your focus to the meeting place of your heart. Let your heart fill with the concern. Working with just this meeting place, consider how you are feeling now. What are the emotions that are stirring in you? What are the emotions below the first layer of emotion? And below that layer?

Now, bring your focus to the meeting place of your body. Let your body speak to you now. Working with just this meeting place, what is your felt sense of this concern?

Where in your body are you responding to this? What does that place in your body have to tell you?

Now, bring your focus to the meeting place of your soul, that part of you that connects you to the sacred. The language of the soul sometimes speaks through metaphor and symbol, color and image. Consider your concern. What color or image springs to mind? What symbol might represent this concern? What is the situation like?

Now that you have been present to yourself in all four meeting places, what insights have you gained? Which meeting place provided the most information? Which meeting place provided the least?

When you become regularly present to yourself in all four of the meeting places, your ability to be present to others, the world, and the Divine expands. It is the difference between being a rosebud and a full blooming rose, a closed or open door, a brook or the ocean.

When you practice this with something beautiful, you will find yourself in a deep gratitude practice.

Quotations on Being Present

You are here so this is holy ground
In all that is, you are here.
This is holy ground, the ground of my being now.
My spirit bows to you upon this holy ground. ❧ Monica Brown

The past is history, the future is mystery, and today is a gift; that is why we call it a present. ❧ Eleanor Roosevelt

The Divine is viewed as being outside of time. The Divine sees the past, present, and future as actualized in the present moment, the now of eternity. ❧ Unknown

Presence is a noun, not a verb; it is a state of being, not a state of doing. ❧ Unknown

Children have neither a past nor a future. Thus they enjoy the present—which seldom happens to us. ❧ Jean de la Bruyere

Life is a great and wondrous mystery, and the only thing we know that we have for sure is what is right here, right now. Don't miss it. ❧ Leo Buscaglia

Life is a succession of moments. To live each one is to succeed. ❧ Coretta Kent

Living in the moment means letting go of the past and not waiting for the future. It means living your life consciously, aware that each moment you breathe is a gift. ❧ Oprah Winfrey

Present moment living, getting in touch with your "now," is at the heart of effective living. When you think about it, and the future is just another moment, you can live. Now is all there is, and the future is just another present moment to live when it arrives. One thing is certain; you cannot live it until it does appear. ❧ Wayne Dyer

Don't let the past steal your present. ❧ Cherralea Morgen

No yesterdays are ever wasted for those who give themselves to today. ❧ Brendan Francis

Questions on Being Present

1. Which quotation on being present most speaks to you?

2. What does being present mean to you?

3. How do you live in the "now"?

4. What gets in the way of you being present to yourself, to others?

5. As a guide, how do you help the traveler be present, experience presence?

Response to Questions on Being Present

1. Which quotation on being present most speaks to you?

The quotation, "The past is history, the future is mystery, and today is a gift; that is why we call it a present" makes me think that Eleanor Roosevelt was a mystic in her own way. It is the best example of why being present is so right on.

2. What does being present mean to you?

It means showing up, being in the now, stepping out of the past and not worrying about the future. It is about seeing every moment as precious and rich and holy in itself. It is about living in the now.

3. How do you live in the now?

By slowing down, taking time, looking around, smelling the roses. It is about making time for quiet, having sabbaticals regularly, going on retreats, being in nature, and freeing oneself of anxiety and worry—and admitting they have no redeeming value.

4. What gets in the way of you being present to yourself, to others?

Expectation of others, my fear of disappointing others, needing to please, getting caught up with things, being busy saving the world, failing to notice what is right in front of me. And most important, not noticing the graced moments and the holiness in everything.

5. As a guide, how do you help the traveler be present, experience presence?

I help the traveler by creating a safe space for the traveler to have time to feel, to pray, and to sit quietly. Giving the traveler opportunities to notice what is right around him or her, having them name where they have experienced the holy in his or her life and allowing for creativity and imagination to be a part of the time together.

Chapter Six

Listening

After one has created a safe place and been present as the traveler or the guide, then begins the next important piece, which is listening.

This process is both a way of being and an action. It is truly an art form.

Listening is the act of hearing attentively; "You can learn a lot by just listening."

To make good music, one needs to give it a hearing, to listen.

Others words for listening are:

- hearing
- auscultation—listening to sounds within the body
- sensing, perception—becoming aware of something via the senses
- rehearing, relistening—the act of hearing again.

All of these are important actions in the listening process.

There is an art to listening. The guide must remember it is the art of listening, not the art of being silent. There are times that call for being silent and times that call for listening to the traveler's story and the spirit's guidance. Remember, the art of listening involves the three key areas on the spiritual journey:

- Creating a safe space
- Being present
- Listening

The key to this is that listening results in engagement; it is about connection and relationship.

How does the guide arrange the time in order to listen well and stay connected to the traveler, and how can the traveler listen well to the guide? This is more complex than might meet the eye.

The following seven components can help the guide and traveler to listen to and stay connected to each another.

1. Prepare self and the safe space
2. Welcome
3. Opening
4. Check-in—self, not agenda
5. Story (the traveler's story)
6. Direction
7. Ending

First, the guide prepares by creating the space, being present, freeing him- or herself from whatever is on his or her mind. It is very important that the guide be present to the traveler and be open to inner and external guidance. This means being open to listening to the Spirit with a whole heart, soul, mind, and body.

Second, the guide welcomes the traveler. Hospitality is very important in this work. It sets the tone that allows the traveler the space in which to proceed.

Third, a guide offers some kind of opening that helps the traveler become centered and be in the moment, into present time. The guide can begin with silence, with a prayer, with a poem, with a piece of art, or anything that helps the traveler free him- or herself from distraction.

For example, the following prayer by Jay Daniel is something the guide often uses:

In this century and in any century,
Our deepest hope, our most tender prayer,
Is that we learn to listen.
May we listen to one another in openness and mercy.
May we listen to plants and animals in wonder and respect.
May we listen to our own hearts in love and forgiveness.
May we listen to God in quietness and awe.
And in this listening,
Which is boundless in its beauty,
May we find the wisdom to cooperate
With a healing spirit, a divine spirit,
Who beckons us into peace and community,
Into creativity and laughter.
We do not ask for a perfect world,
But we do ask for a better world.
We ask for deep listening.

Fourth, the guide asks the traveler how he or she is, what is on his or her mind at the present moment. Check-ins can be done verbally, nonverbally, or in a creative way. Just ask how the traveler is; have the traveler check in by drawing where he or she is on a sand tablet or choosing a feeling word from a set of cards. The key point of this exercise is to keep it brief, and make sure it is about the traveler and not an "agenda item" for the guide.

Fifth, the traveler is asked to share what he or she wants to talk about; what piece of the story does the traveler want to share at this time? Be sure to allow enough time to do so.

Sixth, the guide then shares what he or she heard, asks questions, or gives the traveler a direction. This is not done out of curiosity; it is not a time to explore the guide's curiosity, but to help the traveler on the journey. Asking the question "WAIT" (Why am I talking?) is a great reminder at this point in the session.

Seventh, it is important to bring the time together to a close. The traveler will be leaving the guide and going out on his or her own, so it is important not to leave the traveler in a vulnerable place. This step is called an "up and out." It brings the traveler back to actual time.

Being together as guide and traveler is not about just hearing. It is about noticing all that is said—*and* what is not said. The guide listens without an agenda, without expectations or a need for what the guide thinks the outcome should be. It is not listening out of curiosity. It is listening with appreciation, reverence, and gratitude. There are some definite "don'ts" in this process.

The "don'ts" are:

- Don't go to hear.
- Don't have an agenda.
- Don't question just for information.
- Don't act out of curiosity.
- Don't give homework, unless it is asked for.
- Don't be a listening partner by just remaining silent.

*"We were given two ears but only one mouth, because
listening is twice as hard as talking."*

The "do's" are:

- Be present.
- Listen well.
- Ask questions.
- Guide.

- Be supportive.

Expressing wants, feelings, thoughts, and opinions clearly and effectively is only half of the communication process needed to establish a deep relationship between the guide and traveler. The other half is listening and understanding what the other communicates. When a traveler decides to communicate with the guide, he or she does so to fulfill a need. The traveler wants something, feels discomfort, and/or has feelings or thoughts about something. In deciding to communicate, the traveler selects the method that he or she believes will effectively deliver the message to the guide. The method used to send the message can be either verbal or nonverbal. When the guide receives a message, then undergoes a process of interpreting it and understanding it—meaning takes place. Effective communication exists between the traveler and guide when the guide interprets and understands the traveler's message in the same way the traveler intended it. This is central to the traveler and guide's relationship. The traveler gets to share using whatever form of communication is safe, and the guide has the privilege of listening for both the mode of the traveler's form of communication and the verbal and nonverbal sharing that the traveler offers.

Key areas that may present difficulty for the guide or listener, which can get in the way of listening to the traveler on the journey are these:
- inadequate voice volume or diction that renders difficulty in hearing
- not being focused
- repetitive talking, rather than storytelling
- too many details being provided
- too many topics being discussed at one time
- body language that is contradictory to the words
- narration that results in losing the point
- more concern being given to the listener than what is being said
- the use of phrases or words that are not understandable, which can block the process
- letting feelings of fear, anxiety, or embarrassment lead the conversation
- forgetting to take the time to honor clear thinking
- forgetting to honor whatever feelings are being shared

Some key areas that are helpful to the listener or guide are these:
- being free from an agenda

- being patient, waiting for an opportunity to share
- verifying or giving notice that the guide has heard the speaker
- being present as the listener, by giving good attention through body language
- occasionally saying back what the guide has heard, to support the speaker and let the traveler know the guide is present and listening
- listening for the form the traveler is using to communicate (for example: storytelling, art work, ritual, prayer, metaphors or symbols, facts, beliefs or points of view, feelings)

As a guide, the listener attends to the traveler from wherever the traveler is coming. The purpose and the nature of the relationship with the traveler usually determine what is appropriate and important for this special time together.

There is a real distinction between merely hearing the words and really listening for the message. When listening effectively, the guide understands what the traveler is thinking and/or feeling, from the traveler's own perspective. It is as if the guide were standing in the traveler's shoes, seeing through the traveler's eyes, and listening through the traveler's ears. The guide's own viewpoint may be different and may not necessarily agree with the traveler, but as the guide listens, he or she understands from the other's perspective. To listen effectively, the guide must be actively involved in the communication process and not just listening passively.

The guide always wants to act and respond on the basis of the traveler's understanding, but sometimes there is a misunderstanding of which neither person is aware. With active listening, if a misunderstanding has occurred, it will be known immediately, and the communication can be clarified before any further misunderstanding takes place. This helps prevent pitfalls down the road.

Several other possible benefits occur with active listening. Sometimes the traveler just needs to be heard and acknowledged before she or he is willing to consider an alternative or soften his or her position. It is often easier for a person to listen to and consider the other's position when the traveler knows the other is listening and considering his or her position.

The guide always works at becoming a more effective listener. The guide practices active listening techniques—and this becomes a regular practice.

Reflection on the Art of Listening
by Peg Edera

The *Art*—creative, unique expression, connective, engagement, evolvement, not about mastery. Expand this concept all the time.

Of *Listening*—to traveler (directee), to self, to God, to the language of the heart and soul. How do we do this simultaneously (multi-tasking listening)?

Listen to traveler for: his or her truth (how does she or he recognize this?), joy and lightness of being, movement and stuck-ness, the longing, the call, the relationship with God, God's presence, the dreams, the danger, the deepening, the metaphors and archetypes, what he or she loves, the fears, humor, compassion, the judgments, how he or she lives, what is missing.

Listen to self for: the truth, the humor, what is hard and what is easy, what the body says (the rise and fall of energy), when the traveler needs help, when the directee needs help beyond spiritual direction, compassion, generosity, love, discernment, judgments, intuitive understanding including: alarms, connections, archetypes, and metaphors, the voice of God as the traveler knows it.

Listen to God for: truth, guidance, metaphor and humor, the voice, wisdom, knowing, clarity, compassion, love, discernment.

Listen to the language of the heart and soul for: metaphor, symbol, color, poetry, query rather than answer, possibility, love, compassion, the blending of emotion and intellect, discernment, spaciousness, wisdom from the Saints, prophets, poets, Holy Books, etc.

How does one do this?

Ask for guidance—hear with wisdom and love, speak with wisdom and love.

Practice listening—*Lectio Divina*, meditation, sensory inventory, listening and journaling, silence, practice, practice, practice. Meet the directee in that "field beyond right and wrong." Suspend the need to have an answer. Suspend the ego.

Know the triggers—then the traveler needs to ask for guidance.

Know the boundaries—then the traveler needs to ask for help.

Quotations on Listening

Love mystery—Listening has no ultimate achievement. Our capacity and ability changes daily, hourly, by the minute, and by the second. A good day can be followed by one full of distraction and ego. Forgive yourself and open your ears and heart again. ❧ Anonymous

Spend time every day listening to what your muse is trying to tell you. ❧ St. Bartholomew

We do not believe in ourselves until someone reveals that deep inside us something is valuable, worth listening to, worthy of our trust, sacred to our touch. Once we believe in ourselves we can risk curiosity, wonder, spontaneous delight, or any experience that reveals the human spirit. ❧ e.e.cummings

Set up the listening. Prepare who you are talking to for what you want them to hear. Get people to listen as a possibility rather than a problem. ❧ Mal Pancoast

The world is full of people that have stopped listening to themselves or have listened only to their neighbors to learn what they ought to do, how they ought to behave, and what the values are they should be living for. ❧ Joseph Campbell

When I don't like a piece of music, I make a point of listening to it more closely. ❧ Florence Schmitt

Years ago, I tried to top everybody, but I don't anymore. I realized it was killing conversation. When you're always trying for a topper you aren't really listening. It ruins communication. ❧ Groucho Marx

Music is the effort we make to explain to ourselves how our brains work. We listen to Bach transfixed because this is listening to a human mind. ❧ Lewis Thomas

Questions on Listening

1. Which quotation on listening most speaks to you?

2. How do you feel when someone truly listens to you?

3. How do you feel when you listen well to someone else's story?

4. What gets in the way of you listening to someone else?

5. What is it like to listen to yourself?

Response to Questions on Listening

1. Which quotation on listening most speaks to you?

"Spend time every day listening to what your muse is trying to tell you," speaks to me because I have spent so much of my life listening to others tell me what I should or shouldn't do. But working with my guide has helped me realize I have my own truth, and I have a body, heart, soul, and mind to guide me. I also have a muse that speaks loud and clear when I make time to listen.

2. How do you feel when someone truly listens to you?

I feel honored, respected, and valued. It makes me feel that I have something worth saying and that I have a story that is important enough to be told and be heard.

3. How do you feel when you listen well to someone else's story?

I feel it is a privilege and an honor to be in the presence of someone sharing their story, putting their joys and struggles in words and in discovering that what they say is worth listening to.

4. What gets in the way of you listening to someone else?

I sometimes want to share my story that relates to the traveler's story, and I sometimes want to help them, fix them, or give them advice instead of just listening. I sometimes don't give them enough time to feel the feelings before I give them a direction or ask a question. I am learning that listening is often enough and certainly is the beginning of any good relationship between a guide and traveler.

5. What is it like to listen to yourself?

It has been very hard in the past, because I was so judgmental and hard on myself. I didn't know how to forgive myself, and I held on to lots of anger and resentment. I also often focused on the wrong question. Having a guide has helped me share my own truth and trust myself. I listen much better.

Chapter Seven

Telling One's Story

Telling one's story is the real work of the spiritual journey. In telling one's life story, the traveler gives attention to his or her history, the developments, the struggles, the social identities, the joys, the places where the traveler has moved, and the places where he or she is stuck. The traveler also reviews the persons, places, events, and feelings that brought the traveler to where he or she is now and that help the traveler to see what is working and what still stands in the way of going forward.

To go on a spiritual journey means choosing to take on the questions, stirrings, and movements that will deepen the connection to one's self, the universe, and the Divine.

The three key elements (creating a safe place, listening, and being present) are central for the guide in participating in the traveler's story.

For the traveler to go on a spiritual journey, he or she must be able to listen to what is stirring within, what the call is, and what the heart is saying. The traveler needs to notice, pay attention to, and make time to listen to the questions that are coming forth in life.

For the guide, this is the central part of the work. The guide listens to what the traveler has to say and pays good attention to the story. The guide does not set out an agenda or try to determine where the traveler needs to go. The guide, in listening to the traveler's story, notices where the stirrings occur and helps the traveler determine the best direction to go on the journey.

The second key element is *being present*. The traveler has to be present to what is taking place in the here and now. It is always easier or more comfortable to stay in the past, to stay where it is known and comfortable, free of risk. Or the traveler can focus on the future, on what could be or where he or she wishes to be. But to go on a spiritual journey, the traveler needs to begin at the starting line, in the present moment, and to pay good attention to where the present moment is and where it might be calling. It is important to let the traveler begin where he or she needs to begin.

For the guide, being present is the key to being faithful to the traveler's journey. The guide is open to what is taking place in the moment, what the traveler is saying, and what the traveler is bringing to the session.

The spiritual journey is the development of the individual's inner life.

Meditation on Telling Your Story
by Peg Edera

Find a quiet corner. Sit on the floor, a cushion, or a chair. Keep your feet on the ground.

When you are comfortable, breathe deeply. Feel the breath go all through your body. For three or four breaths, inhale deeply and exhale slowly and completely. Exhale slowly and completely.

Write about any or all of the following questions:

- What is the story you are most longing to tell?

- What is the story you have never told?

- Recall listening to a friend telling you an important story about his or her life. What was stirring in the story? What stirred in you as you listened?

- Recall telling a friend or counselor an important story about your life. What happened when you were deeply heard? What happened when you realized they understood what was in the story below the details? How did you feel? If you do not recall being heard in this way, imagine what it might be like, how one might feel. Write about the possibilities of the experience.

Quotations on Telling One's Story

To stay in one place and watch the seasons come and go is tantamount to constant travel: One is traveling with the earth. ❧ Marguerite Yourcenar

Stripped of all its outer encrustations, spirituality emerges as a science, as scientific as any other, as verifiable in its results. Let any seeker take it up and let him create in the laboratory of the soul the conditions that are prerequisite; as sure as the day follows the night shall he rise into the Kingdom of God. ❧ Sant Kirpal Singh

If we do our job well in telling our story, I think we'll be all right. ❧ David Glass

We are all called to share our story, it is our gospel. ❧ James Galluzzo

Each of us has our own unique story to tell. Some stories are, of course, more dramatic than others, but the fact remains that each of us has a story that is unlike anyone else. Our life experiences are uniquely personal to us, and because they are personal, they are also stories that we tell with both passion and conviction.

There is great power in the telling of your story to someone else. When we talk of where we have been and our own personal journey, God's power is powerfully revealed in our lives. His presence in the mountain heights and deep valleys of life is put on display. His helping hand in times of trouble is clearly seen as being present, in and through our own experiences.

When you tell your story, it is an encouragement to those who hear it. Sadly, all too often we keep our stories to ourselves, because we fear being transparent with those around us. When we hold back our experiences from others, we are depriving them of the strengthening that our story would bring.

As Christians we have been called to "bear witness" to the work of Jesus in our lives. Telling our stories is a key part of our ongoing witness to those who are yearning for His touch. ❧ Carl Willis

You will be his witness to all men (and women) of what you have seen and heard.
  ❧ Acts 22:15

Questions on Telling One's Story

1. What is the "telling your story" quotation that most speaks to you?

2. How was it sharing your story for the first time?

3. How was it for you to hear someone else's story?

4. What part of telling your story is connected to your spiritual journey?

5. Have you thought about writing your gospel and sharing your journey with others? How would you begin?

Response to Questions on Telling One's Story

1. What is the "telling your story" quotation that most speaks to you?

The Acts 22:15 quotation speaks to me. I strongly believe that in telling one's story, we are bearing witness to our piece in creation; we are beginning to see our connection to the world.

2. How was it sharing your story for the first time?

We are all called to share our story, it is our gospel. I didn't believe I had a story worth sharing, and now I am working on writing my gospel. I do have good news to share.

3. How was it for you to hear someone else's story?

It was challenging. I always felt like I was too intense, so I held back. It wasn't until I was forty-one that I found someone whom I trusted and who listened to me. It was truly a liberating moment and changed my life.

4. What part of telling your story is connected to your spiritual journey?

Only in telling my story did I realize that my truth is much more important. It helped me break away from other people's and institution's stories that I tried to fit into and that never felt comfortable. Once I had the courage and safety to share my story, I was able to connect to my value and qualities and was able to start to live out of my story.

5. Have you thought about writing your gospel and sharing your journey with others? How would you begin?

Yes, I think about it often. I would begin by owning that I was born fully human and deeply connected to all people and to the universe. It would begin with, "In the beginning, I was fully human, good, loving, and loveable, and I went forward in life discovering what it meant to be fully human and connected."

Chapter Eight

Bearing Witness

The fact that a traveler has chosen to go on a spiritual journey is the first sign of bearing witness. The traveler makes the decision, and that speaks loudly to self and to others. The traveler overcomes the fear and anxiety by deciding to go on the journey without knowing exactly where it will lead.

Bearing witness is noticing and affirming what is true, genuine, and authentic. Bearing witness gives testimony to the truth and to authenticity by helping the traveler give witness to the authentic self.

The guide starts from the premise that the traveler is a human being who is good, worthy, loveable, and capable. The guide does this even if the traveler is not connected to the authentic self, or if the traveler has been conditioned away from the true self because of unhealed hurts and old messages from family, society, or religion.

The role of the guide is to bear witness to the courage demonstrated by the decision to begin the journey.

Together the traveler and the guide model interdependence on the quest.

As guide for the traveler, the guide is actually being a witness to the traveler's story, to the life, to the truth as it occurs—to the struggles, joys, and delights and to the changes, transitions, and discoveries that happen along the journey.

This happens as the guide bears witness to his or her own story and embraces the sacred in life. As the guide bears witness, travels on the journey, asks questions, and listens for movement, he or she embraces the essence of being a guide. If the guide is not on his or her own spiritual journey, the guide should not be guiding others.

The guide bears witness by creating a safe space, by being present, by listening both to and for the guide and to and for the traveler. Because this is about a spiritual journey, one bears witness to the holiness that is experienced as the guide and as the traveler and gives attention to the gratitude of sharing and experiencing the holy.

As the guide bears witness, the results of this special relationship between guide and traveler are many: connectedness, love, mutuality, compassion, trust, acceptance, safety, and openness. These results then grace the lives of the relationships that exist outside of the guide and traveler's time together. And this leads to bearing witness to all connections and to bearing witness to the world, to the cosmos, to the holy in everyone and all of creation.

Meditation on Bearing Witness
by Peg Edera

The act of bearing witness opens a channel for healing. When the truth of what occurs to you is seen, heard, or affirmed by another, the truth begins to take root. When your experience is grounded by the witness of another, doubt, blame, resentment, and self-criticism begin to crumble. The light of witness pulls even the darkest events into the possibility of healing.

It is a serious and sacred act to bear witness, to say, "Yes, this is so." When we exclaim the truth of the experience of another as it occurred to them, we help them claim their truth at that time. That claiming may be the Mother to acceptance, release, forgiveness, and/or transformation.

Journal Exercise

Recall a time when you witnessed for another person. Perhaps you said, "That is a horrible thing that happened to you. No one deserves such treatment." Or you may have said, "What a beautiful thing you did. That was so heartfelt and strong."

- What occurred?
- What difference did you make to that person?
- How did you feel?

Recall a time when you witnessed for a cause or issue. Perhaps you campaigned for a political candidate. Perhaps you gathered signatures on a petition. Perhaps you made a speech or marched in a protest.

- What occurred?
- What difference did it make to you?
- To others?
- To the world?

Recall a time someone witnessed to or for you.

- What occurred?
- How did you feel?
- What difference did it make to you?

Do you see a relationship to hope and bearing witness? If so, what is it?

Quotations on Bearing Witness

We must bear witness. ❧ Elie Wiesel, (Written on the wall of the U.S. Holocaust Memorial Museum in Washington D.C.)

Every artist seems to me to have the job of bearing witness to the world we live in. To some extent, I think of all of us as artists, because we have voices and we are each unique. ❧ Jane Rule

This we can all bear witness to, living as we do, plagued by unremitting anxiety. It becomes more and more imperative that the life of the spirit be avowed as the only firm basis upon which to establish happiness and peace. ❧ Dalai Lama

That which was from the beginning, which we have heard, which we have seen with our eyes, which we have looked upon, and our hands have handled, of the Word of life; (For the life was manifested, and we have seen it, and bear witness, and show unto you that eternal life, which was with the Father, and was manifested unto us;) That which we have seen and heard declare us unto you, that ye also may have fellowship with us: and truly our fellowship is with the Father, and with his Son Jesus Christ. ❧ 1 John 1: 1–3

Great comforts do, indeed, bear witness to the truth of thy grace, but not to the degree of it; the weak child is oftener in the lap than the strong one. ❧ William Gurnall

But when the Comforter is come, whom I will send unto you from the Divine, even the Spirit of truth shall testify of me; and you also shall bear witness, because you have been with me from the beginning. ❧ John 15: 26–27

No matter what our achievements might be, we think well of ourselves only in rare moments. We need people to bear witness against our inner judge, who keeps book on our shortcomings and transgressions. We need people to convince us that we are not as bad as we think we are. ❧ Eric Hoffer

Questions on Bearing Witness

1. Which quotation on bearing witness speaks to you?

2. Recall a time you witnessed for another person.

3. Recall a time you witnessed for a cause or issue.

4. Recall a time someone witnessed your truth.

Response to Questions on Bearing Witness

1. Which quotation on bearing witness speaks to you?

The quotation about everyone being an artist speaks to me. I believe everyone has something to share, whether it be in words, art, music, dance, poetry, woodwork, and so forth.

2. Recall a time you witnessed for another person.

I have had the privilege of witnessing someone discover their voice. They had been ignored for so long they had forgotten that they had a voice, and once they discovered it, they were afraid to use it. After being guided through the healing process, they were finally able to start using their voice in our times together. Then they began to practice with others whom they trusted. Now the traveler is guiding others and teaching others to meditate and to practice loving-kindness.

3. Recall a time you witnessed for a cause or issue.

When I was challenged by important women in my life to stand up against sexism, I felt hurt and misunderstood. I was blinded by my own upbringing and male privilege. I first had to notice the sexism all around me and notice where I had been conditioned as a sexist. After working to clean up my own sexism, I committed to working to end sexism by challenging anyone who made a sexist comment, and I made sure that at work and in my personal life I was conscious of being sensitive to inclusive language, inclusive hiring, and inclusive pay.

4. Recall a time someone witnessed your truth.

I still remember the first time someone told me that I had a valued message for the world and a way of thinking and living that needed to be proclaimed. At first I didn't believe it, but slowly I trusted the witness and began to practice telling my message. After four or five years, I have made it the most important work I do in the world.

Chapter Nine

Discernment

Both the traveler and the guide must learn about discernment, because much of listening and guiding comes from discerning what and where a traveler is called to be.

Discernment is the cognitive process of understanding.

It is knowing, it is comprehending, it is self-knowing, it is appreciating, it is realizing, and it is knowing the truth. It is an ongoing process by which the traveler and guide come to a knowing and understanding of his or her truth.

On the spiritual journey the guide and traveler spend a lot of time discerning, listening to the heart, listening to the inner voice, and listening to the Spirit. Discernment is a practice that is important to use throughout the journey.

What Is Spiritual Discernment?

Spiritual discernment is calling on the Divine, the Spirit, or energy to lead or give direction on a matter. It is how the Spirit shows the individual and the community what the Divine wants the traveler and guide to do and be.

Discernment is more than just a skill. Discernment is a gift before it is anything else. Yet there are clearly skills that are put to use in the process, and a guide can become better at discernment through training and experience.

Yet, discernment is more than just a process. Even for the most "material" or "nitty-gritty" matters, there is a Spirit at work nudging, leading, and even pulling. For most "spiritual" matters, there are disciplines, methods, processes, means, and tools that the Spirit can work through to help discern. Discernment isn't usually a sudden "zap" from beyond, but something that emerges from discipline and practice.

These are the main things to look for in discerning about something:

- Discernment is governed by love.
- Discernment centers on movement.
- Discernment invites to be human.

- Discernment gives strength to the individual, the community, and its members.
- Discernment gives power, wisdom, character, boldness, and unity.
- Discernment helps create a love of what is right and a turning away from what is not truly human.

Holy Writings and Discernment

Travelers and guides of many faith traditions turn to holy writings—for example, Scripture, the Koran, the Bhagavad Gita, and Buddha teachings—in order to get one's story right. Holy writings are not there to hold the Spirit in chains. The writings are to be used in the light of freedom, knowing that these ancient words do not directly address all matters. The holy writings can often become guides to movement and inspiration.

Some look at the holy books seeking support, not truth. For others, the patient, prayerful, steady study of holy writings brings many rewards: truth, understanding, clarity, knowledge, movement, and growth. The Spirit rewards such discernment by developing within each traveler and each guide an understanding of what is true.

The traveler relies on that truth when he or she reads the writings in earnest prayer. The Spirit wants the traveler to study, to trust, and to shape life according to what is good, to steep it into the soul, to live by the framework and the world vision of peace and justice.

Stories and holy writings shape an authentic Spirit-led experience and set the guidelines. Then the traveler looks for the course and purpose of what the Divine is sharing.

Like everything else in this world, the results of discernment are bound by imperfections and thus can be false, or shallow, or merely mistaken. But it helps greatly to have a good foundation, holy writings, and the right attitude, and to share the discernment with someone else.

Discernment is fully in line with the spiritual journey of questions, stirring, movement, decision, and action.

Meditation on Discernment
by Peg Edera

Discernment practices we recommend:

❖ Asking for guidance from God, the Divine, the invisible realms, the Transcendent Other

❖ Reading the signs

❖ Quaker process of Clearness Committees

❖ Looking for the Fruit of the Spirit

❖ Being present to the Four Meeting Places

Reflection Practice

"The work does not need to be grand, only fitting. It is guided by asking ourselves over and over: What is the next right thing? Maybe it is to rest after an arduous project...maybe it is to reclaim creativity...maybe it's to say "yes" or "no" to an opportunity. We have watched each other so many times come alive to the next right thing. Our hearts jump with excitement and we're off...." ❧
Christina Baldwin from *The Seven Whispers*

Sometimes all we can see is one small thing. If we patiently practice this, we are often led to the next thing to do, and then the next.

Today, practice asking yourself: *What is the next right thing?* Pause. Listen. Try this five times today.

Quotations on Discernment

As far as we can discern, the sole purpose of human existence is to kindle a light in the darkness of mere being. ❧ Carl Jung

Discerning and acting on God's will does not mean you'll never have difficult days or feel lousy sometimes. But choosing to live in alignment with God makes you more joyful, compassionate, and peaceful, even on bad days. ❧ Debra K. Farrington

The important thing is not to stop questioning. Curiosity has its own reason for existing. One cannot help but be in awe when he [or she] contemplates the mysteries of eternity, of life, of the marvelous structure of reality. It is enough if one tries merely to comprehend a little of this mystery every day. Never lose a holy curiosity. ❧ Albert Einstein

Nothing discernable to the eye of the spirit is more brilliant or obscure than man; nothing is more formidable, complex, mysterious and infinite. There is a prospect greater than the sea, and it is the sky; there is a prospect greater than the sky, and it is the human soul. ❧ Victor Hugo

Live your questions now, and perhaps even without knowing it, you will live along some distant day into your answers. ❧ Rainier Maria Rilke

Our decisions and our search for guidance take place in the active presence of a God who intimately cares about our life situations and who invites us to participate in the divine activities of healing and transformation. ❧ Frank Rogers, Jr.

Questions on Discernment

1. Which quotation on discernment most spoke to you?

2. How do you define discernment?

3. How do you practice discernment?

4. Can you reflect on a time you had to sit with the unknown and listen to what your heart and the Spirit were saying to you?

Response to Questions on Discernment

1. Which quotation on discernment most spoke to you?

"As far as we can discern, the sole purpose of human existence is to kindle a light in the darkness of mere being." How moving to see my sole purpose as being to experience light in the darkness; what a beautiful thought and a challenge to live out.

2. How do you define discernment?

It takes place when I am not certain, when I am in the state of unknowing, of not having a clear picture or even the right question, or when I am not sure where I am going. Discernment is the process now helping me approach these places of mystery.

3. How do you practice discernment?

I usually bring the confusion to my guide, and he has me talk about where I am and how I feel. After naming it and expressing and discharging effects of the feelings, the guide asks me to sit with the question and listen for what my heart is offering and what is the spirit saying. It is the telling about the issue, dealing with the feelings, and then going into quiet—free of the stuff and the feelings. It puts me in a place of listening. Sometimes the guide offers a question, suggestion, or direction.

4. Can you reflect on a time you had to sit with the unknown and listen to what your heart and the Spirit were saying to you?

I was in a job and working hard and making progress. But it was draining, and I was more and more exhausted. I was honored for the good job I was doing. My head told me I was on the right path and making good decisions, and my heart loved the healing work I was doing for others, and my soul was silent, and my body was worn down.

I brought the issue to my guide. Through the process of discernment I realized I was focusing on the wrong question. I was looking at the issue as "Am I doing a good job?" instead of how it was affecting my well-being. So I had to discern if I was in the right place or if I was ahead of my time or if I was sinking.

After much prayer, self-talk, checking with friends, going to my guide; I decided to resign.

It was a painful, fear-filled, and courageous decision. And I left without a job, without income and new challenges to face. But I knew it was the right decision for my well-being, and it was right for my heart, soul, mind, and body.

Chapter Ten

Being Human

The one thing that is certain on the journey is that whoever calls upon a guide to be there, that traveler is a human being. The guide, embracing the humanity of each traveler he or she meets, treats him or her as fully human, not as a victim or an oppressor. This means that the guide gives attention to the traveler and not to the traveler's "stuff." A traveler is not his or her stuff (fears, old messages, conditioning away from his or her humanity). The traveler is a human being.

Everyone is born human, and his or her humanity is what all have in common. It is the basis for how humans relate to each another, treat each other, resolve conflict, love, forgive, heal, and live in community. Being human calls everyone to be on a spiritual journey because each traveler and guide is an inherently spiritual being.

To be human is to be connected to all men and women, as well as to the planet. If the traveler and guide were truly connected, then the traveler and guide would hold out equality, love, and justice for all. There would be no reason for "one-upmanship." It would mean replacing being politically correct with being humanly connected. If a problem arose, humans would solve it with brilliance, with an innate sense of justice, and with the ability to seek and find the truth. This connection is the base for the spiritual journey and the definition of spirituality: the connection to self, others, the work in the world, the earth, the universe, and whatever is transcendental for each traveler.

Once a person feels a loss of connectedness or does not feel a part of the overall community, the fear, hurt, and isolation leads to holding on to the victim role. Others have expressed it as a slipping into numbness, into a kind of surviving life mode. But numbness or survival is settling for less than being fully living and thus is giving up power in the process. In this state, the traveler acts out of survival or coping mechanisms, trying to be less or more than human.

What does this all mean?

To live life as less than human is to take on the victim role. It is powerlessness; it is a false martyrdom; it is "poor me;" it is a way of giving over and giving up. It is settling for less. Living as less than human gives one the impression that this is the best it gets or can get. The victim plays out helplessness and hopelessness. It is giving up on life as it can be, a life full of living, a life settling for nothing less than everything. And being less than human gives the oppressor a role that grants a false sense of power; it is manipulative; it is controlling; it is abusive; it is disrespectful. It is avoiding humanity, so one can avoid another's humanness. It is name-calling; it is stereotyping; it is threatening; it is bullying; it is putting others down. It is claiming power at another's expense. It is about power plays. It is getting what one wants by manipulating, by not being human.

Both the victim and oppressor roles stir up fear, isolation, pretense, and/or settling for less than a full life. The traveler buys into scarcity by believing there is not enough love, resources, time, and so on, so the person figures out a way to get it first. The traveler goes for self-interest rather than for a unique place in human interest. Unfortunately, somewhere along the line he or she loses the meaning of connection—or it was never held out in the first place. The sense of community and the place in community seems to have gotten lost or, at the least, misplaced.

Human liberation is being free of the roles of oppressor or victim. It is living free of any form of conditioning that leads away from inherent humanness. It is about life and nothing less than full humanity.

This information is based on Charlie Kreiner's theory that everyone is one human species. Every man and woman, young and old, every ethnic group, every class, every creed, every way of life, every community is seen as fully human.

Charlie Kreiner points out six characteristics regarding being human. These are that a human being is universal, permanent, whole and complete, limitless, unconditional, and unique.

Humanity means all, everyone. It is universal. These qualities are true for all human beings, not just the ones who are similar or who think the same. It includes everyone, even the ones a person doesn't like or can't figure out. When a traveler thinks he or she is not good enough, he or she feels "less than" and sees only the weaknesses. The traveler, with the help of the guide, must tell him- or herself that he or she is fully human and must try hard not to get defensive or act less or more than human toward others. The guide helps the traveler by reminding him or her to look at his or her humanity. This helps the traveler live a life free of distress, guilt, shame, and past mistakes and instead live life as it is meant to be—fully alive.

Being human is permanent; it can never be taken away. It exists as long as the guide and traveler are breathing. It has a permanence that gives power, hope, and the strength to get up every morning and say yes to a new day. This is a wonderful part of being human, especially when it feels hopeless or impossible. Humanity contradicts the worst feelings. There is a power in being human, in living in the human community. What a great delight to realize that although the traveler might feel like he or she has lost some human qualities, those qualities are still there under the hurt. It is through the guide reaching out to the traveler, listening, and allowing the traveler to discharge, that enables him or her to let go of what has gotten in the way of being fully alive. Then the traveler can see the permanence of his or her inherent human qualities. Every traveler is born with all the inherent human qualities. Once he or she has support and can participate in the healing process, he or she can reclaim their inherent humanity.

Humanity is whole and complete from birth. The traveler or guide doesn't become "more" human as time goes on. A child of two days and a sixty-two year old are both fully and completely human. An old person might have more life experience, but every infant is fully human at birth. Every infant possesses all the human qualities as part of his or her birthright. Color, gender, and/or physical abilities do not lessen or strengthen one's humanity. This is an important concept to understand. If the guide could see the humanity in all the travelers at every age as whole and complete, then adultism and ageism would be eliminated. Both the traveler and guide would claim the innocence of children. This doesn't mean being childish; it means reclaiming the child's ability to go for what he or she wants: the right to be held, to be loved, and to have attention in the present. Children can just crawl right up into a person's lap when they want to be close. A child knows specialness, connectedness, and love. Adults want this also. However, being "sophisticated," one often gets what one wants without asking, through power plays, withdrawing, isolation, fighting, and whining. Many adults would rather be right than happy. And adults have so much trouble asking for help. Sometimes adults don't even know what is needed, so they shut down or search in all the wrong places. But adults don't have to do this. Adults are human, fully and completely. Adults need to reclaim this part of self. It hasn't gone away. It feels lost only because of past hurts or because no one was there when the person needed help.

Humanity is also limitless. The traveler and guide do not "run out" of being human or "use up" their humanity. Human qualities are not like a glass of water that gets emptied. But a traveler often feels that way. It seems at times that there is no more patience, no more ability to love, or no more hope. A person feels mistrust of another person, can't laugh anymore or can't think straight. Life certainly can feel like that at times, but it is only a feeling. (There is a big difference between feeling good and being good.) It is the distress (physical or mental suffering, pain, anxiety, or sorrow) that gets in the way of limitless humanity. It is the opposite of rose-colored glasses. The world is the same but, if one looks at it through distress-colored glasses, it looks different. A person knows that when he or she is in a good space, then the person is much more tolerant, patient, and understanding. When filled with agitation, anxiety, and stress, one can't seem to think clearly, and becomes impatient, judgmental, and very unsocial. So, feelings get in the way, but that doesn't put limits on humanness. It might feel like the mind can't take any more, but in reality, there is so much more potential. Humanity has even more possibilities because it has no limits. The more the traveler and guide love, the more he or she trusts, creates, and connects; the more humanity can flourish, the more participation there will be in community, and thus the more one will live life to the fullest. This is the abundance that flows forth like grace when a person is open to movement.

Humanity and all human qualities are unconditional. The traveler or guide doesn't earn humanity. It is a birthright; it is freely a part of who each person is from birth. A person doesn't have to be someone or do something to be a human with human qualities. There are no "ifs," "ands," or "buts." Everyone is human. This means that each person is unconditionally human. Distresses, unhealed hurts, fears, or other behavior might not seem very human, but such feelings do not make the traveler or guide less human, regardless of the struggles with life. No matter what, each traveler is inherently good: has a right to exist, is loved, is intelligent, and so forth. A person's right to exist and all the other inherent human qualities are unconditional. Sometimes a child is defined as "good" because he or she doesn't cry, or flushes the toilet, or cleans his or her room. But these things don't make someone good. The child is inherently good. Children don't have to prove it or earn it. A person doesn't have a right to exist just because she or he has a college education, or is from a first-world country, or is young, or is able-bodied. A person isn't loved only if he or she has a lover or if she or he has had sex. A person has a right to be loved simply because being loved is an inherent quality. A woman or man isn't intelligent if she or he beats out another in an SAT test, or is a CEO, or is the President. A person is unconditionally intelligent; it is one of the inherent human qualities.

Last, humanity is unique. If the guide and traveler accept the first five characteristics: universal, permanent, whole and complete, limitless, and unconditional, one might think all human beings are the same. But the characteristic of uniqueness also posits that each person lives out her or his humanity in her or his own special way. There are seven billion ways. Each person's history, culture, spirituality, and life experiences play into the uniqueness. What a wonderful world it will be when each person's uniqueness is seen as a gift! What a rich and exciting world will exist! Instead of arguing that men are more violent and don't feel, or that women are too emotional and can't think or lead clearly, or that children need to be spoken for, or that blacks are not as intelligent as whites, or that Hispanics don't work as hard as Anglos, or that the physically challenged are not creative, intelligent, strong, or sexual, what if instead of all this misinformation, stereotypes, and narrow visions of anyone who is different, the common humanity in everyone was recognized? The guide and traveler would see all the inherent human qualities in everyone, and discover and honor all the unique ways each person lives out humanity, each individual adding to the conscious whole. Each person could discover how every group is filled with a rich diversity. How exciting and fascinating and delightful to discover the traveler's own way and be open to the unique way of each person. What a world! Thus, the obligation is for each person to step out of fears and hurts and be an example of this new humanity, which is really who each person already is.

Inherent Human Qualities

Charlie Kreiner holds out this model as a framework to look at human nature.

There is one species, which has two genders: female and male. All females and all males are fully human. Common humanity is what connects all. A human arrives on this planet endowed with qualities that define the person. These qualities are inherent human qualities. There are several hundred inherent human qualities that fall under the six characteristics.

Every guide and traveler is inherently good, loving, loved, loveable, kind, just, peaceful, compassionate, social, connected, interdependent, communicators, learners, healers, thoughtful, artists, emotional (all feelings), thinkers, teachers, dreamers. These are just a few of the multitude of human characteristics. Guides should make a list and have the traveler name these inherent qualities. Guides will always want to work with the inherent qualities that the traveler presents in his or her story.

When the traveler and guide are present to self and living life fully, then the traveler and guide are connected to these inherent qualities of being human.

Reflection on Being Human
by Susan Hammond

Being human is:

- living with a non-dualistic mindset
- identifying the layers of old messages and traumas and letting them go
- being aware of my passions, dreams, and desires for life and then taking steps forward to actualize them
- accepting the imperfectness of my humanity

I have always thought I must be perfect to be fully human. I also know I am not perfect and cannot be. Accepting the non-perfectness of me is hard as stone. Perhaps the stone, now, is beginning to crack.

New thoughts emerge. New feelings emerge. I do not have to be perfect. I laugh more, learning to be more like Mr. Chuckles (Jack, my husband). I can work in the garden and quit when I am tired. The yard can be messy and not perfect. The house, too, does not need to always be picked up. I do not have to please others. I can please myself by going to bed early, buying books to read, practicing my walking, snuggling with Sheba, my dog. I can disagree with Jack in a nice way rather than in an adversarial way. I can say no. I can say yes. My goal is to do no harm to others, and other than that, I am free to live. But I may not know how.

I am letting go more and more. It has taken me a long time to arrive at this place. I am letting go of those old thoughts, letting go of control over Jack, letting go of expectations for myself, letting go of pleasing others, and letting go of needing others' approval. As each letting go is practiced and done, it seems I am getting lighter. There is less to carry: less responsibility, less doing, a shorter To Do list, more time to watch the hummingbirds outside my kitchen window and make sugar water for them, more time to find what I like to do, discovering some of the fun things I have forgotten all about or have wanted to do but never took time to explore.

Being human is letting myself be all of those facets of me without regret or apology to others or myself; those facets, in part, include: the responsible one, the one who organizes, the Martha one, the Mary one, the fun one, the laughing one, the serious one, the one who does everything, the one who does nothing, the one who writes, the one who helps others, the one who is letting go, the one who keeps seeking, the one who keeps changing. And, it is my choice which ones appear, when and for how long. But being human, mostly, is my awareness of maintaining this multifaceted person in balance and in harmony with Life.

Reflection on Being Human
by Maureen Schwerdtfeger

For me to be fully human means I live my life to the fullest—with a little extra gift.

My saying this, however, involves more than just being. By living to the fullest, I am connecting my mind, heart, body, and soul in everyday being. My mind is constantly thinking through situations and making decisions. I use my gut feeling to come to some of the conclusions. I have found when I open my heart and let the Divine in, my intuition and final decisions turn out for the best.

I am paying more attention to the care of my body lately. My body is a temple of the Divine and should be in the best physical condition as possible in order to carry out God's plan for me. Taking care of my body has involved adjusting my diet and adding some exercise. I enjoy walking the paths in the parks. I have become more aware of the beauty surrounding me with the use of my senses: eyes, ears, smell, taste, and touch. I am finding that a walk down the paths and/or around the labyrinth helps with my thinking and decision-making.

By using my mind, heart, body, and soul, the making of decisions and physically carrying them out has made me aware of whom I am. Instead of being the quiet person that does not speak or act out her beliefs, I now trust in the Divine and can be open and share my beliefs and thoughts with others. There are no mistakes, but I am learning many lessons. My experiences have been many—from joy to sorrow to the awesome awareness of the Divine in my life.

The extra gift that lets me be fully human came when I began seeing others as human and created by the Divine. Whenever possible, I give a hug, using both my arms and eye contact to show my love for the other human.

Quotations on Being Human

Live your life from your heart. Share from your heart. And your story will touch and heal people's souls. ❧ Melody Beattie

A human being is part of a whole, called by us the Universe, a part limited in time and space. He experiences himself, his thoughts and feelings, as something separated from the rest, a kind of optical delusion of his consciousness. This delusion is a kind of prison for us, restricting us to our personal desires and to affection for a few persons nearest us. Our task must be to free ourselves from this prison by widening our circles of compassion to embrace all living creatures and the whole of nature in its beauty. ❧ Albert Einstein

Love is the essence of human experience and emotion. It is at the root of all and everything we, as humans, do. Without love, what do we have to live for? ❧ Unknown

It is only when you have both divine grace and human endeavor that you can experience bliss, just as you can enjoy the breeze of a fan only when you have both a fan and the electrical energy to operate it. ❧ Sri Sashay Say Baba

To do something, however small, to make others happier and better, is the highest ambition, and most elevating hope, which can inspire a human being. ❧ John Lubbock

Success, happiness, peace of mind, and fulfillment—the most priceless of human treasures—are available to all among us, without exception, who make things happen—who make "good" things happen—in the world around them. ❧ Joe Clock

The human contribution is the essential ingredient. It is only in the giving of oneself to others that we truly live. ❧ Ethel Percy Andrus

Questions on Being Human

1. Which quotation on being fully human most speaks to you?

2. Where do you see yourself as fully human?

3. Where is it hardest for you to live out of your full humanity?

4. What helps you see each person as fully human?

Response to Questions on Being Human

1. Which quotation on being fully human most speaks to you?

"To do something, however small, to make others happier and better, is the highest ambition, and most elevating hope, which can inspire a human being."
This speaks to me because it is small acts and kindnesses that are the most powerful way of helping the traveler to experience human to human connection. And it is through that connection that the traveler can connect to his or her own inherent humanness.

2. Where do you see yourself as fully human?

When I laugh, when I embrace my gifts, when I am connected, when I recognize who I am, when someone loves me, when someone touches my heart, and when I step outside of the old messages of not being enough or of trying to be perfect.

3. Where is it hardest for you to live out of your full humanity?

When I am in the church or any other institution that doesn't honor my gifts or doesn't recognize that the spirit speaks to me also, I feel discounted. When I have to hold back and not be myself, when I am not allowed to speak my truth, and when people are being mistreated and I am the lone voice to speak up for them, and I get afraid.

4. What helps you see each person as fully human?

When I recognize each person as a child of the light, as a child of God, as being inherently good, that is when I see his or her humanity. And knowing that I am connected to every person, human to human, whether I feel it or whether or not they act in a human way.

Chapter Eleven

Living Life Fully

Living life fully is a great model for the spiritual journey. The journey is filled with excitement, with adventure, with challenges, and with being authentic. Living life fully means being free of anything that gets in the way of living fully. It is about human liberation.

Remember that the guide and travelers are fully alive. Both are human and both are connected to self, others, and the universe. The question, then, is: Are both up to the call to be human, to be free of anything that gets in the way of being fully alive? Or, does the traveler want to continue to whine, to complain, to blame others, and to believe that life sucks? This hinders the journey.

This chapter holds out ideas on what it means to live as a human. It looks at humanity, human nature, community, and liberation. It looks at how liberation allows humans to achieve true destiny, living life fully in present day reality and beginning the journey. This part of the journey is the liberation piece, the discovery of change, stirrings, questions, and movement. The guide plays a big part in noticing the change, movement, and liberation. The guide does not want to fix, or be in charge, or have his or her own agenda.

This chapter is the true work that the traveler and guide do together and are constantly practicing. It is the practice of being human and living life fully. It is:

- liberation from all things that cause one to be less than human or more than human
- liberation from anything that disconnects one from any person or any form of life on the planet
- a way of thinking and a way of living
- liberation that leads to connection to true self
- knowing that there is someone else who cares and listens
- about connection
- about community building

This model challenges the traveler to take the journey outside of past emotional hurts, conditioning, and the effects of so much misinformation handed down. It shows how those hurts are established and presents a healing model. It is both personal and social, helping the traveler to be alive in the world instead of scared to go out into the world.

If the guide and traveler accept humanity and the humanity of all others, regardless of race, creed, class, gender, age, physical ability, or sexual orientation, then he or she can stand up and model it for the entire world to see. Each human being is looking for life, some desperately, insanely, and addictively—others hopefully, patiently, and openly as learners in life. If a traveler can live on the basis of his or her inherent humanity, instead of based on past emotional hurts, conditioning, and the effects of misinformation handed down to him or her, then the guide can be a contradiction to the injustice and oppression brought on by sexism, adultism, racism, classism, ageism, homophobia, and anything else that challenges humanity.

Human liberation calls on the traveler and guide's inherent humanity to live life fully, in the moment, basing life solidly on inherent humanity. This allows him or her to re-experience life in the present reality. And this means a person can think, feel, decide, and act based on inherent nature and can make the journey to being a healthy human being. Liberation is the result of the traveler and guide working together, offering a new way of seeing, noticing, thinking, and being. It is being free from anything that gets in the way of being the traveler's authentic self.

What is human liberation?

What is the meaning, the power, the history of this word, *liberation*?

Liberation is deeply rooted in ancient worlds, in pagan and religious traditions. It is a central piece to Jewish history. It is a part of countries and cultures such as Central and South America, Africa, Ireland, Tibet, and Hong Kong.

Liberation is a central piece in every major movement: the civil rights movement, the GLBT movement, the women's movement; it is essential; it is the foundation for a spiritual journey. The traveler and guide build this foundation through establishing safety and trust.

Human liberation emerges from the lived experience, not of an individual traveler, but rather the combined experience of many travelers. A traveler who is born inherently free, who was once oppressed but struggled to become free again, has been liberated through his or her work and the support of others. The traveler knows being free is who he or she is. It is true that individuals have experiences but live in relationship, in connection to others, because of healing and moving toward liberation in community.

All liberation starts from an analysis, the examination of a story that is both personal and social, whether it comes out of the traveler's home, community, nation, or the planet. This analysis or new way of looking (looking out of freedom and humanity) comes from awareness that prejudice, oppression, injustice, and the marginalization of any group is not part of being inherently human. It is conditioning that reduces or minimizes humanity.

Therefore, this new awareness leads to a reorientation of human practice, a turning toward the oppressed and listening. This involves modeling a liberated lifestyle for the oppressed through listening partnerships and through active support. (Listening partnership is the process used by two or more people as a way of assisting the traveler to explore and begin healing from the distress in his or her life, the distress that is usually the result of unhealed trauma from his or her early life and that prevents success today.) When this happens, there is a rediscovery of humanity in creating a more just, liberated society worthy of human beings.

From this freedom and human view, the guide and traveler can begin to see new things:

- a new effort by the community to form a social conscience, free humans who recognize that all humans can always feel, think, decide, and act on inherent human nature.
- a blossoming of communities being allies to each other
- an addressing of the needs of the community in creative ways
- a new and active participation and listening to all groups, beginning with those who have been denied a voice in the past
- an organizing of groups to address the misinformation and to envision new ways of claiming humanity free from fear, prejudice, and conditioning

This new way of looking, the liberation viewpoint, enables humanity to begin to break the cycle of oppression and to move the traveler toward claiming his or her freedom.

(The cycle of oppression is the model in which one begins life as fully human, then early unhealed hurts affect the person; reactions and behaviors continue the oppression, caused by misinformation and behavior based on that misinformation; then the cycle is broken by getting correct information, healing

old hurts, and changing reactions and behaviors that support living one's life as fully human.)

Once liberation is reclaimed, the connection to humanity is reestablished and engagement between and among takes place. There is no place in liberation for the victim role (*the conditioned role based on misinformation that an individual or group can be less than human, less than another human or group of persons; a role based on helplessness and powerlessness*) and no place in liberation for the oppressor role (*the conditioned role based on the systematic, one-way, physical, psychological, economic, or religious mistreatment of one person or group by another or by a member of another group or by society as a whole; a role based on power over people, manipulation, bullying, feeling "more than" human).*

Engagement is being, working, and connecting together. This is what takes place between the traveler and guide. When the guide and traveler are engaged and connected, the guide does not treat the traveler as if he or she doesn't have the answer. Instead, the guide and traveler engage with each other; no power over, no hierarchical model, no "I have the answers," no rescuing. The guide and traveler believe in the "power with" model, seeing and using each person's gifts.

True solidarity, with liberation between the guide and traveler, is found in the act of love, in the praxis of love toward all.

Quotations on Living Life Fully

To stress the need for liberation means that we see the ongoing development of humanity in a particular perspective and in terms of a specific philosophy and theology of history. It means that we see it as a process of human emancipation, aiming toward a society where men and women are truly free of servitude, and where they are the active shapers of their own destiny. Such a process does not lead us simply to a radical transformation of structures—to a revolution. It goes much further, implying the creation of a whole new way for men and women to be human. ❧ Gustav Gutierrez

Whether they are followed or not, the pathways opened up here lead into a long and unforeseeable future. The only thing that can be said is that they take their cue from flesh-and-blood human beings who are struggling with mind and heart and hand to fashion a life out of the human materials of our great but oppressed continent. ❧ Juan Luis Segundo

The lens of women's flourishing focuses faith's search for understanding in feminist theology. It does so in the context of myriad sufferings resulting from women being demeaned in theory and practice in contradiction to the creative power, dignity, and goodness that women appreciate to be intrinsic to their own human identity. When this suffering is brought to consciousness, when its causes are analyzed, when dangerous and therefore suppressed memories of women's agency are brought to light, and the praxis of resistance and hope are begun, then conditions exist for a new interpretation of the tradition. Feminist theology results when women's faith seeks understanding in the matrix of historical struggle for life in the face of oppressive and alienating forces. ❧ Elizabeth A. Johnson

Questions on Living Life Fully

1. Which quotation about Living Life Fully most speaks to you?

2. Where have you experienced liberation, the freedom to live fully in your life?

3. Where have you experienced someone else's liberation?

4. Have you had to break the cycle of oppression in your life or helped another break the cycle of oppression?

Response to Questions on Living Life Fully

1. Which quotation about Living Life Fully most speaks to you?

"To stress the need for liberation means that we see the ongoing development of humanity in a particular perspective and in terms of a specific spirituality and theology of history." This is my favorite quotation because it talks about the ongoing development of humanity from a spiritual perspective.

2. Where have you experienced liberation, the freedom to live life fully in your life?

When I finally decided that being gay was OK. What a freeing experience for me. No longer did I have to worry that someone would find out, no longer did I have to live a secret life, no longer did I have to live a lie to be safe. My guide was central in helping me embrace who I was and to step out of the fear of being hurt for who I am.

3. Where have you experienced someone else's liberation?

I watched a black man being harassed and continually discriminated against all his life. He was the only black student in an all white high school. When he went off to college, he was so afraid and shut down. He decided to seek out a guide who helped him face his fear and heal from years of discrimination. After working with his guide for three years, he slowly began to embrace his authentic self as a human being who is a black man. Through education and practice, he stood up for himself and began to reconnect with being a proud black human being.

4. Have you had to break the cycle of oppression in your life or helped another break the cycle of oppression?

When I stood up for gay rights during two ballot measures I was verbally and physically attacked. But I realized that what the gay and lesbian community was asking for were basic rights. They were fighting for the right to jobs, housing, and friendship. It seemed so obvious to me that people's fear, misinformation, and lack of information were preventing the general populace from honoring basic human rights. So as a human being I felt called upon to connect with a group of people who were being oppressed and to ask them how I could help them in the fight for human rights. They called on me to speak out and to let the groups of people who were in my life to know the injustice that had taken place for too long.

Chapter Twelve

Spirituality and Diversity

Every person is given the opportunity to go on a spiritual journey. There is no traveler who is eliminated from being offered this chance. So the spiritual path offers the most diverse gathering, probably more than any other place. This is because every person on the planet is inherently spiritual, and every person has the qualities of curiosity, growth, discovery, and connection. People of every race, culture, orientation, gender, and physical ability can go on a journey. There is no emotional, physical, sexual, religious, or cultural handicap that would prevent anyone from going on a spiritual journey.

The challenge in this area is for the guide. Can the guide be present to anyone and everyone who comes to the journey? Can the guide be open to someone who is radically different from the guide or who is journeying on a completely different path? The answer should be yes, but everyone has his or her places of being stuck, and the guide has to be honest with him- or herself and the traveler in telling the truth. Not being able to guide someone allows the guide to look at the area where he or she might be stuck, might not understand, or might be prejudiced. It also offers the guide an opportunity to look at what is missing in his or her life, or in what areas he or she lacks information or is holding on to misinformation.

There is a process for both the traveler and the guide to help clean up any misinformation or prejudice that might get in the way of building trust. Remember, prejudice is based on misinformation or lack of information. The process involves looking at the stereotypes of any given group, then comparing those stereotypes to the qualities inherent in every person. Next, you speak to the group you are looking at: men, women, people of color, people of another tradition, sexual orientation, ablebodiness, and so forth. These are called social identity groups—groups based on race, creed, age, place of origin, orientation, physical ability, nationality, urban or rural influence, class, or economic status, to name a few.

Ask:

- What are the stereotypes about the group?

- What would the group like others to know?
- What does the group never want to hear again?
- What feelings come up when the group hears the list of stereotypes?

The last question, about the feelings that come up, is the place where the real work has to be done. The feelings that emerge when any group is treated unjustly are very similar. The effects of the feelings of hurt, shame, anger can begin to be cleaned up by facing, feeling, and healing the feelings and the effects of the feelings.

Example of this Process from a Class on
Diversity taught to Hispanic and Anglo Persons

An example of the process and exercise that the traveler works on in the spiritual direction training is as follows.

- What are the stereotypes?
- What would the group like others to know about Hispanics?
- What does the group never want to hear again?
- WHAT FEELINGS COME UP IN THE GROUP?

Example: Hispanic Community and the Anglo Community

Stereotypes of Hispanics
Lazy, dirty, illegal, weak, macho, stupid, sexist, Catholic, tardy, overly pious

What would the Hispanics like others to know about them?
Don't group all Hispanics as the same.
We are very diverse.
We are loyal.
We come from many countries.
We support our families.
We work hard.

What does this group of Hispanics never want to hear again?
That Hispanics are lazy and cannot be leaders.
That we don't have a work ethic.
That we are weak.
That we all have the same beliefs and rituals.
That we don't have any morals.
That we are stupid or not educated.

What feelings come up from the group when the group sees the list of stereotypes?
Anger, fear, sadness, disappointment, hurt, mad, afraid, isolated, bitter, misunderstood, judged unfairly, seen as all alike

Stereotypes of Anglos

Privileges, responsible for all the problems, have all the power, are racist, control institutions, have all the money.

What would the Anglos like others to know about them?

All Anglos can't be grouped together.
Anglos come from all over the world.
Many were immigrants.
We work hard.
We struggled to learn the systems.
Some of us are poor, most are middle class, and some of us are wealthy.

What does the group of Anglos never want to hear again?

That we are the oppressors.
That we have all the power.
That we are the cause of all the world's problems.
That we are anti-civil rights for other groups.
That our lives are easy.

What feelings come up from the group when the group sees the list of stereotypes?

Anger, misunderstood, resentment, sadness, fearful, disappointment, hurt, afraid of people different from us, separated, need to hide, judged unfairly.

What each group can relate to are the feelings that the others express, and it is such feelings that the traveler and guide can face, feel, and heal so that they can connect to others.

Quotations on Spirituality and Diversity

We need to give each other the space to grow, to be ourselves, to exercise our diversity. We need to give each other space so that we may both give and receive such beautiful things as ideas, openness, dignity, joy, healing, and inclusion. ❧ Max de Pree

We all should know that diversity makes for a rich tapestry, and we must understand that all the threads of the tapestry are equal in value no matter what their color. ❧ Maya Angelou

I feel my heart break to see a nation ripped apart by its own greatest strength—its diversity. ❧ Melissa Etheridge

If we cannot now end our differences, at least we can help make the world safe for diversity. ❧ John Fitzgerald Kennedy

I take as my guide the hope of a saint; in crucial things: unity, important things, diversity; in all things, generosity. ❧ George Herbert Walker Bush

Questions on Spirituality and Diversity

1. Which quotation on diversity most speaks to you?

2. How do you see diversity as a gift?

3. What social identity group is most missing in your life?

4. What social identity group has most graced your life?

5. How do you overcome conditioned or taught stereotypes about a social identity group and then reconnect to the humanity of that group?

6. What is the relationship of spirituality and diversity?

Response to Questions on Spirituality and Diversity

1. Which quotation on diversity most speaks to you?

"We all should know that diversity makes for a rich tapestry, and we must understand that all the threads of the tapestry are equal in value no matter what their color," by Maya Angelou says exactly what I believe about diversity and why I have devoted my life to honoring diversity.

2. How do you see diversity as a gift?

Each new social identity group I have encountered in my life has enriched my life through their stories, their way of thinking, their way of living, and their way of expressing themselves. How boring life would be if we lived with people just like us. We would miss the rich opportunity for diverse foods, cultures, philosophies, beliefs, ways of living, and ways of loving.

3. What social identity group is most missing in your life?

People who are fundamentalist, because they often condemn others in the name of love. I have to work very hard to see them as fully human. I know they are, but they make it hard for me to embrace them, and I make it hard to embrace them because of my judgment.

4. What social identity group has most graced your life?

Women. They have been there for me, encouraged me to embrace my creativity and sensitivity. They have protected me and stood up for me. They have been my best teachers and the givers of hope in my life.

5. How do you overcome conditioned or taught stereotypes about a social identity group and then reconnect to the humanity of that group?

Through education, overcoming misinformation about the group, connecting with them, cleaning up my own prejudice and fears with help from my own social identity group (not expecting the group I have stereotyped to clean up my stuff).

6. What is the relationship of spirituality and diversity?

If we are open to traveling the spiritual path, we will encounter spiritual writings from various traditions, a variety of spiritual practices from many sources, diverse belief systems, and amazing people who have so much to offer.

Chapter Thirteen

Healing

Some say that a traveler has to clean things up before he or she can go on a spiritual journey. This is not true. As a traveler goes along on the journey, anything that needs to be cleaned up will surface. Others say some travelers are afraid to go on the journey because the traveler will be challenged, will have to take risks, and will have to face old hurts or be hurt. All of the above will happen, but the traveler will be able to meet the challenges along the way and will not have to face things alone—because the traveler has chosen a trusted guide.

When talking about healing on the journey, the guide is not taking over the work of doctors or therapists. The guide focuses on the healing that needs to be done or assisting the traveler in reconnecting to her- or himself (heart, soul, mind, and body), to others, to the world, to the universe, and to the Sacred.

The things that get in the way of pursuing the traveler's spiritual journey are the same things that play a big part in getting in the way of humanness. These six things are used by society in many forms to try and block a traveler or guide from claiming his or her inherent nature and to perpetuate discrimination, prejudice, and alienation.

Charlie Kreiner calls these areas the "Big Six." Once examined, the guide and traveler can see how they affect the journey, how hurt happens, how hurdles block human qualities, and how feelings from the past seem to prevent the guide and traveler from being fully human. Each traveler needs to face these issues, feel the feelings, deal with the effects, heal from the past hurts, and live life fully in the present.

The first of the "Big Six" is ISOLATION.

Isolation is defined as "being set apart; a place away from others, a person with a communicable disease; to remove from others; to obtain an element in an uncombined state; to cause to stand alone, separated, detached, or unconnected with other things or persons; to insulate, to cut off from all contact with others; to make solitary."

Isolation is the most commonly used adult "power play." Adults often withdraw or isolate to avoid facing issues, feeling feelings, or moving forward with healing. Isolation is a way of coping with unhealed feelings and unresolved issues, and it leads to feelings of loneliness, detachment, separation, and being set apart from others. Isolating oneself seems very effective, because by staying disconnected, it feels like hurt can be avoided—yet it also prevents connection.

Isolation is not the same as making a decision to take some quiet time alone; rather, it is a distress pattern (old hurts formed into a pattern that gets in the way of the traveler's humanity), a way of avoiding self or others. Isolation can also be a punishment (for instance sending a child to her room when she misbehaves). But is this an effective way of helping a child resolve a problem or heal from a mistake or hurt? The traveler does not heal alone. She or he heals when the traveler has a guide available to support the traveler by being an ally. Often, early training sets up the way a person does or does not relate to others. Isolation is a patterned response to early events in a person's life.

When no guide is present for a child—when there is little or no emotional support—a child learns to protect him- or herself early on. When the child chooses isolation as protection, then the child hides who he or she is, hides the vulnerable side that was hurt or not supported, and holds in the true feelings for fear of judgment or getting hurt. Even though isolation makes a traveler feel safer, the numbness eventually causes stress by preventing the person from being who he or she really is. Every form of isolation is distress. Isolation is always a distress recording (a pattern of behavior that is based on the traveler's distress), not a reality. If isolation were truly better, the traveler would accept isolation with no discomfort or disequilibrium. But this doesn't happen; the distress seems and feels bigger than it is.

A person who isolates often believes that there is no place in the world to go for help, so he or she goes inside. The person is alone. He or she gives up on the inherent human quality of connectedness, gives up—or sometimes hasn't experienced or recognized—connectedness. The person doesn't trust others, doesn't ask for help, and doesn't express feelings. The traveler works hard to do things alone and wants others to rescue him or her. He or she sabotages any attempt at real connectedness because of fear. In reality, no guide can move another out of isolation. It must be the traveler's decision, and the traveler needs the support of the guide.

A colleague of mine is an incredible minister. She deeply challenges each person to claim goodness. But I have never heard her claim her own voice around her own goodness. I came to see that being for others was her way of isolating. She has been deeply hurt and has chosen service to others as her drug of choice for isolating. She does many good things, but stays disconnected from herself and others.

The traveler can contradict isolation by making a decision to step out of the past and live in the present, believing each person is there to help and believing in his or her own ability to heal. The traveler who isolates perceives everything as fine or everything as hopeless. He or she does not see that there is a great array of choices in between. Isolation allows the feelings of powerlessness, loneliness, and hopelessness to run wild. A traveler is not responsible for his or her early hurts, but is responsible for healing the effects of how he or she was hurt. This is how the traveler grows, evolves, and moves out of the past into the present time.

The contradiction to isolation is connectedness, love, interdependency, hope, trust, intimacy, and living in the present as a social human being.

The second of the "Big Six" is REJECTION.

Rejection means "to refuse to accept, recognize or believe; to cast away as worthless, to set aside, to throw away; to refuse to acknowledge, adopt, or believe in."

All of these meanings play out in this pattern of coping. Rejection is the refusal to be connected, the refusal to accept affection or help from others; it is the giving over of power to others, which leads to isolation. A person can reject others or be rejected by others only when he or she steps out of his or her humanity. When you are connected to humanity, rejection is less likely. Rejection leads to feelings of invisibility, inadequacy, inferiority, low self-worth, and guilt. If these feelings are acted upon—with the result that one builds walls for protection, keeps from achieving or trying to go for goals, or acts out of fear—then one's needs, ideas, dreams, and hopes will not be heard and will be rejected. In short, the process will be sabotaged before life has the chance to unfold.

A traveler who takes on this distress pattern (patterned behavior based on his or her own distress) of rejection believes he or she is unlovable and powerless, a feeling that he or she has to make it on his or her own. The traveler lets another take advantage of him, and the feeling is that of being used. A large amount of energy is put out to survive and little is invested in living life fully. This leads to questioning self-worth, compromising values and morals, and blaming inadequacies on others. A traveler acting this way will always feel disappointed and excluded.

Without others, a person will try self-survival or working for perfection (which isn't a human quality), and this reinforces hopelessness and failure, which only continues the patterned cycle. A person who has been rejected continues to be in isolation and keeps him- or herself from human qualities. He or she lives in such distress that he or she often acts out in patterns of blaming self and others, in addictive behavior, in discounting his or her real self, and in desperately trying to replace frozen needs (needs that were never met in the past) with fantasies and danger.

The traveler must stay connected to his or her power and dignity so that no one can hold power over or reject him or her. The traveler will not give the feeling of rejection power in its self.

A person I deeply love is a brilliant, clear thinking woman who challenges each person to go for life. She often holds out new possibilities for others. She is a model with her words and in her actions as examples for others. But because of her own fear of rejection, she ends up getting stuck when she tries to go for life herself. She begins to doubt herself, clings to others to feel validated, and pushes others to take on the hard pieces of leadership. But she is beginning to go for life, is deciding to feel the feelings of rejection, and is choosing a guide who encourages her to validate herself. The guide contradicts rejection patterns by claiming the traveler's connectedness, self-worth, dignity, clear thinking, and power. The guide holds out "power with" and contradicts the victim role by encouraging the traveler to choose life in the present through connection.

The third of the "Big Six" is RIDICULE.

Ridicule is defined as "a pattern of words and/or actions that attempt to call forth contemptuous laughter at or feeling toward a person: to mock, to make fun of, to attempt to arouse laughter or merriment at another's expense by making fun of or belittling a person; the act or practice of making a person or thing the object of jest or sport; humiliating a person, putting someone down, denying him or her; to scorn and to demean the traveler's ability to set and achieve meaningful goals." Ridicule is clearly a power play that starts early on in life with put-downs and name-calling. If it happens enough times or has enough power or terror behind it, the traveler begins to believe the ridicule is reality. There is an equation: "$I \times V = R$," Imagination multiplied by Vividness equals Reality. If someone is told she is stupid, and she hears this in a variety of ways, a number of times, she begins to believe it is real. But it is only pseudo-reality (a self-defined reality based only on feelings). She might feel stupid, but it is only a feeling. She might begin to do stupid things, acting on the feeling; but in reality, she is inherently intelligent. When someone else tries to contradict the original feelings, often the person who feels stupid distorts the information or discounts it. This shows how deeply the traveler has been hurt. The traveler continues to feel the ridicule and believes that he or she can never measure up to the expectations of others.

The experience of feeling ridiculed continues into adult life, setting the person up to experience limitations to his or her ability in the work place, a holding on to sexist and racist myths, a fear of disparaging comments about one's size, race, gender, physical ability, and sexual orientation, and a pattern of pursuing relationships based on need or frozen feelings. Then the feeling of ridicule leads a person to believe the conditioned messages and to act on these ridiculing messages. This effectively prevents the traveler from living up to his or her full potential, from claiming all human qualities, from moving out of the victim role and conditioning, and from healing past hurts. The traveler might claim that ridicule is an external conditioning, and it often is; but the traveler affected by ridicule often submits to verbal abuse and acts out his or her negative feelings of inadequacy by teasing others, by being a bully, by being a clown, by putting self down, or by walking around with a "poor me" attitude or a martyr complex.

A great woman leader was constantly being ridiculed because she was rather short. For years, she felt she could not be a leader because of her size. In reality, she was tired of being laughed at for being less than five feet tall. A few years ago, she began to proclaim her power. She asked her allies to help her claim her voice and to stop the ridicule around her size. For a while, she made tall men kneel in front of her so they could look up to her. She doesn't do that anymore, because she now claims her dignity in being a short woman leader and has retained her power. Her voice is clear, strong, and tall!

In summary, the contradiction to ridicule is self-love, being authentically human, claiming the qualities of dignity, goodness, truth, honesty, clear thinking, the right to exist and unconditional love, then viewing and interacting with others in like manner.

The fourth of the "Big Six" is ABANDONMENT.

Abandonment is defined as "being deserted, left behind, forsaken; to give up wholly, to surrender or give over; a complete giving up to drive or cast off, to give up to the control of another; to banish, to give up by leaving, withdrawing, ceasing to be connected."

The pattern of abandonment seems so powerful because of the false power behind its meaning. Abandonment denotes a complete giving up, especially of things people have previously held an interest in, believed in, or were responsible for.

When a guide abandons other human beings or creatures, he or she withdraws support, deserts the traveler, forsakes, and disconnects. This can be done both physically and emotionally. When a child experiences feelings of abandonment, he or she is likely to have difficulty forming close relationships with others. Abandonment becomes a person's coping mechanism for dealing with life's stresses. In adult relationships, a person will feel the same fear she or he did as a child. A word, a tone of voice, a gesture, can drive the person to manipulate others in a way that will prevent a friend or lover from leaving. The person either sets up unhealthy, dependent relationships or sabotages any relationships that hold out true connectedness. The message of fear serves to reinforce the message that says, "I will never be acceptable to another human being as I am." The possibility of being abandoned again seems greater than the pull to connect in a healthy way. This is only distress; it is not reality. It leads to the belief that a person can only be loved by being a pleaser, by being accommodating, and by being dependent. The person feels that he or she can't share his or her thinking because it might be different from another's, and the other will withdraw love, support, and approval. The distress pattern of abandonment leaves the person with the strong fear that others will leave and a feeling of "it's my fault." It is difficult to believe the guide will really be there, because of the strong feeling of abandonment.

In a battered women's group, each woman constantly alleged that it felt better to be in a battered relationship than to be abandoned. Each woman's fear and hurt has allowed the patterns of abandonment to rule her life. The women then learn to work on trusting and connectedness to others and begin to see another choice that does not include abandonment or being battered. The choice is to be fully human and connected to self and others, and choosing to separate if necessary, avoiding abandonment by not playing the victim role.

In other words, the contradiction to abandonment is trust in humanity, trust in self, community, clear thinking, interdependence, and the inherent human qualities of loving, being loved, thoughtfulness, closeness, and being connected.

The fifth of the "Big Six" is THREATS OF VIOLENCE.

The term "threats" is defined as "exerting pressure upon, to urge, press, promise punishment, reprisals or other distress; holding out by way of menace or warning; an expression in words, actions or gestures with the intention to inflict pain, injury or punishment."

Threats are a very effective way of controlling and intimidating others, if the other gives away his or her power and doesn't have a supportive person around. A child tends to believe threats of violence and is told he or she will be hurt even more if he or she tells anyone what has happened. The child is told that if he or she does not keep silent, the threats might come true. So a child learns to stuff feelings, hold secrets deeply inside, make past hurts and the effects of past hurts a part of present life. The child feels suspicious and has difficulty in trusting others and forming open intimate relationships. He or she learns to be a pleaser, out of fear. He or she feels compelled to act in certain ways to be safe and doesn't let anyone really know her or him because others might discover that the pain would be too intense for anyone to handle.

Such fear and guilt of rejection or discovery rules the traveler's life. Resentment and hostility are natural consequences when the traveler behaves only to satisfy others' expectations rather than his or her own. One feels responsible. "It's my fault. I should have been better." If he or she has no way of trusting, no way of connecting, that person tends to act out in anonymous ways that enable him or her to feel close, but never really experience true closeness.

So many abused children have kept silent, stuffed the pain and fear because of threats of violence. Threats have a "power over." When the child, sometimes not until adulthood, is loved, the child begins to remember the abuse and to heal by telling his or her story. In reality, it is the silence that kills, not the threat.

The guide and traveler contradict threats of violence by being connected, by supporting, healing, loving, trusting, having courage and power, and believing in the right to exist in a fully human way.

The last of the "Big Six" is VIOLENCE.

Violence is "exerting physical force for the purpose of violating, damaging or abusing another human being physically, sexually or psychologically, or stopping a person from healing and changing his or her life or from empowering others."

Violence is the unjust inhuman exercise of power and control. It is unjust and inhuman because it exercises power over another individual.

Physical force causes submission of another person. It makes the person do something or go somewhere against his or her will. It causes pain—physically, emotionally, and spiritually.

Sexual force causes sexual intercourse or some other sexual activity to occur by means of physical force, by means of a threat of force, or by use of a weapon. This is sexual abuse and may constitute rape. It violates someone else's body, showing a total disregard for that person's humanity.

Psychological violence is essentially a systematic attempt to control another person's thinking, feeling, and/or behavior. The aim of this kind of violence is to damage the person's sense of self-worth by trying to make her or him a victim and by trying to make the person feel powerless.

Whether a traveler is directly victimized, witnesses the violence, or only hears about it, this experience is very terrifying, confusing, and potentially damaging to the traveler's psychological and intellectual development. He or she feels helplessness, anger, shame, frustration, and distrust. The traveler tends to blame himself or herself, feels his or her innocence has been taken away, and struggles with touch, intimacy, and closeness. Often, this lasts for a long time or until the feelings of hurt are addressed.

The cycle of violence often continues on, perpetrated even by the person who was victimized, because that is what he or she has learned—yet it is a false sense of power and connection.

Violence has a long list of consequences. Growing up in a violent environment can be very traumatic and can leave deep wounds that follow a person throughout life if he or she doesn't have a guide who is offering a hand in healing from the effects of the violence. An abused person tends also to disown part of him- or herself and either becomes aggressive or withdrawn, compulsive or inhibited. An abused person often has an explosive temper, fear of intimate relationships with both genders, and difficulty in setting boundaries. The abused person may often think of self as contaminated or less than whole.

Violence is not always the result of abuse. It can come from old hurts or misunderstandings that seem to have power over one's life. The residue of unhealed pain can control a person's image of his or her self and dictate how the person allows others to treat him or her.

Certain situations can bring up the unhealed pain, and as a result, the person acts out this old anger in violent ways in adult life. In addition to these intense feelings, one's own childhood experiences may contribute to harmful attitudes about self and relationships. A person turns to alcohol or drugs to numb the intense unhealed pain. Others learn the art of disassociation (separating from present reality) in order to cope and survive. But this isn't living fully, and it denies the permanence of the inherent human qualities.

So, the traveler must contradict the woundedness caused by the violence with tenderness, courage, touch, healing, intimacy, love, reverence, innocence, love of one's body, connectedness to the earth, and a deep sense that who the traveler is can never be taken away by anyone.

The guide's responsibility is to offer contradictions to any of the "Big Six" that the traveler has experienced. This helps the traveler heal from the hurt and disconnection and reconnect to humanity.

Meditation on Healing
by Peg Edera

One of the Spiritual Direction practices of healing is to work with the soul. When we work with the soul, we work in the territory of metaphor and symbol. In this exercise, let the work of metaphor help heal your soul.

Examine the "Big Six": Isolation, Rejection, Ridicule, Abandonment, Threats of Violence, and Violence. Choose one and write a brief story in the third person about it. Think of this as a fairy tale or myth. It can closely resemble a personal experience, or it can be a brand new creation. Trust the process and healing will begin.

For example: Ridicule and Rejection

She was born into a family that attended the Church of Disdain every day. Religion was for the unimaginative. God was only an idea fit for the weak and foolish. It was the opiate of the masses, and they were better than any of that. She had inklings, though, inklings of something wonderful that had nothing to do with this family diatribe. To turn her back on these inklings was like turning away from food. The further she turned away, the weaker she felt. The more she heard her family, the more exhausted she became. The day she finally turned away....

Quotations on Healing

You can clutch the past so tightly to your chest that it leaves your arms too full to embrace the present. ✌ Jan Glidewell

Living the past is a dull and lonely business; looking back strains the neck muscles, causing you to bump into people not going your way. ✌ Edna Ferber

The past is never there when you try to go back. It exists, but only in memory. To pretend otherwise is to invite a mess. ✌ Chris Cobbs

Waste not fresh tears over old griefs. ✌ Euripides

The past is a guidepost, not a hitching post. ✌ L. Thomas Holdcroft

The Past is the textbook of tyrants; the Future the Bible of the Free. Those who are solely governed by the Past stand like Lot's wife, crystallized in the act of looking backward, and forever incapable of looking before. ✌ Herman Melville

No yesterdays are ever wasted for those who give themselves to today. ✌ Brendan Francis

Although the world is full of suffering, it is also full of the overcoming of it. ✌ Helen Keller

Eventually you understand that love heals everything, and love is all there is. ✌ Gary Zukav

Healing may not be so much about getting better, as about letting go of everything that isn't you—all the expectations, all the beliefs—and becoming who you are. ❧ Rachel Naomi Remen

If I find a green meadow splashed with daisies and sit down beside a clear-running brook, I have found medicine. It soothes my hurts as well as when I sat in my mother's lap in infancy, because the Earth really is my mother, and the green meadow is her lap. ❧ Deepak Chopra

I had no idea that mothering my own child would be so healing to my own sadness from my childhood. ❧ Susie Bright

Having spent the better part of my life trying either to relive the past or experience the future before it arrives, I have come to believe that in between these two extremes is peace. ❧ Unknown

Questions on Healing

1. Which quotation on healing most speaks to you?

2. Where are you most challenged at embracing your humanity fully, being at one with yourself?

3. When you have been hurt, when your humanity has been challenged, when you have been put down, ridiculed or attacked for your beliefs, how does it make you feel?

4. How do you reconnect to your authentic self?

5. Which of the Big Six has most emerged in your past?

6. As a guide, how can you help the traveler face, feel, and heal from misinformation or disconnection from his or her authentic self?

Response to Questions on Healing

1. Which quotation on healing most speaks to you?

The Rachel Naomi Remen's quotation was my favorite. For me, healing is truly about letting go of anything and everything that gets in the way of being who I am. This quotation says it so well. I believe that when we are whole, holy, good, fully human, we are at one with our authentic self.

2. Where are you most challenged at embracing your humanity fully, being at one with yourself?

The need to please is very challenging for me. I put the other person first and often stuff my own feelings, thoughts, and hopes. The wanting everything to be peaceful for others often leads to denying myself, my own needs, and this leads to resentment.

3. When you have been hurt, when your humanity has been challenged, when you have been put down, ridiculed or attacked for your beliefs, how does it make you feel?

The feelings that most emerge for me are sadness, loneliness, disconnection, hopelessness, fear, and shame.

4. How do you reconnect to your authentic self?

I search out people, places in nature, spiritual readings, and music that remind me of who I really am. Then I make space for myself to experience it and embrace it.

5. Which of the Big Six has most emerged in your past?

Isolation is the one that most affects me, and I use it as a way of coping or avoiding. When I get scared, when I don't feel safe (which is often), when I am afraid, I isolate, so that I will not get hurt again. My heart has been broken too often. I know that isolation is always a form of distress, but I still go there often. I want to break out of the isolation pattern. I am doing that by practicing solitude instead of isolation.

6. As a guide, how can you help the traveler face, feel, and heal from misinformation or disconnection from his or her authentic self?

I would create a safe place and then allow the traveler to talk about the areas in his or her life that prevent them embracing true self. Then I would remind the traveler that he or she never was disconnected. From there I would have the traveler share where he or she got stuck and have the traveler feel the feelings that come up, and then give a direction that would help the traveler reconnect to his or her true self.

Chapter Fourteen

Forgiveness

Forgiveness is a central part of the spiritual journey. The guide has to be able to forgive him- or herself and others if he or she is going to ask the fellow traveler to do the same. A person has to forgive so he or she can reclaim his or her full self. Forgiving is really the process of giving. If the traveler is burdened by old mistakes, by old hurts that have either been caused by or handed to her or him, then the traveler cannot focus on the present moment and will be stuck in old hurts and unhealed pain.

Forgiveness is an important practice and process for both the guide and the traveler.

Forgiveness is typically defined as the process of ceasing to feel resentment, indignation, or anger for a perceived offense, difference, or mistake and ceasing to demand punishment or restitution. The concept and benefits of forgiveness have been explored in religious thought, the social sciences, and medicine. Forgiveness may be considered simply in terms of the person who forgives, in terms of the person forgiven, and/or in terms of the relationship between the forgiver and the person forgiven. In some contexts, forgiveness may be granted without any expectation of compensation and without any response on the part of the offender. In practical terms, it may be necessary for the offender to offer some form of acknowledgment, apology, and/or restitution—or even to just ask for forgiveness—in order for the wronged person to believe him- or herself able to forgive.

Most world religions include teachings on the nature of forgiveness, and many of these teachings provide an underlying basis of forgiveness. Some religious doctrines or philosophies place greater emphasis on the need for a human to find some sort of divine forgiveness for his or her own shortcomings; others place greater emphasis on the need for humans to practice forgiveness of one another; yet others make little or no distinction between human and/or divine forgiveness.

Hinduism

The concept of having or performing atonement from one's wrongdoing and asking for forgiveness is very much a part of the practice of Hinduism. Karma is a sum of all that an individual has done, is currently doing, and will do. The effects of those deeds actively create present and future experiences, thus making one responsible for one's own life and the pain in others. Krishna said in the *Bhagavad Gita* that forgiveness is one of the characteristics of one who is born for a divine state.

Islam

Islam teaches that God (*Allah* in Arabic) is "the most forgiving," and is the original source of all forgiveness. Forgiveness often requires the repentance of those being forgiven. Depending on the type of wrong committed, forgiveness can come either directly from Allah or from one's fellow human who received the wrong. In the case of divine forgiveness, the asking for divine forgiveness via repentance is important. In the case of human forgiveness, it is important to both forgive and to be forgiven.

Christianity

Forgiveness is one of the main themes of Jesus' teaching. He teaches us to pray, "Forgive us our sins as we forgive others." According to Jesus' teaching, forgiveness is something one does so the person can have a clean heart. One is to love God with all one's heart, soul, mind, and body. If one holds resentment or unhealed hurts in one's heart, then one is not able to love with all one's heart. The church honored this message and also called each person to reconciliation, to forgiving the other person so peace could be achieved.

Judaism

In Judaism, if a person causes harm, but then sincerely and honestly apologizes to the mistreated individual and tries to rectify the wrong, the hurt individual is religiously required to grant forgiveness: "It is forbidden to be obdurate and not allow oneself to be appeased. On the contrary, one should be easily pacified and find it difficult to become angry. When asked by an offender for forgiveness, one should forgive with a sincere mind and a willing spirit. Forgiveness is natural to the seed of Israel." (Mishnah Torah, Teshuvah 2:10)

In Judaism, one must go to those one has harmed in order to seek forgiveness.

Jews observe the Day of Atonement—Yom Kippur—on the day before God makes decisions regarding what will happen during the coming year. Just prior to Yom Kippur, Jews ask forgiveness of those they have wronged during the prior year (if they have not already done so). During Yom Kippur itself, Jews fast and pray for God's forgiveness for the transgressions made against God, self, others, and the world.

A Course in Miracles

Forgiveness, as the means to remembering God, is the fundamental message of A Course in Miracles. It teaches that forgiveness is not simply the letting go of resentment, but rather forgiveness is awakening to eternal vision and remembering that there is nothing real to resent. Forgiveness is the recognition, the awakening, if you will, to the reality that the separation never occurred in God's eternal reality. Forgiveness removes the blocks to seeing the eternal goodness in, and unity and equality with, another.

Popular Recognition

The need to forgive is widely recognized by the public, but a person is often at a loss for ways to accomplish it. For example, in a large representative sampling of Americans on various religious topics in 1988, the Gallup Organization found that 94% said it was important to forgive, but 85% said outside help is needed to be able to forgive. However, not even regular prayer was found to be effective. Forgiveness is important, and yet little is done to educate a person on what forgiveness is or how to practice it.

Forgiveness in relation to spirituality is about connection.

Forgiveness is a response to an injustice done to oneself, to another, to the community, to the earth, or to the cosmos. One can latch onto the hurt or injustice or can turn to the good in the face of the hurt or wrongdoing. Forgiveness is the letting go of resentment or revenge and instead giving the gifts of mercy, generosity, and love when the wrongdoer does not deserve it. The wrongdoer can be one's self who is hurting self, or the wrongdoer can be someone hurting another. All of these examples lead to disconnection, while forgiveness leads to connection.

When the traveler has hurt or has been hurt, he or she needs to face the injustice, needs to feel the hurt, the anger, and the resentment; then, having discharged the hurt, the traveler can let it go. Only when he or she has let it go is the person able to look at what happened and see what can be learned from it and what can be done about it. Then reconciliation is an option. There is no reconciliation if the other person is not able to accept responsibility for her or his action or if he or she does not wish to let go of the hurtful behavior or the resulting pain. Only if the traveler is willing to do the work, can he or she consider reconciliation. It is important to notice that if it is in any way hurtful or would cause abuse, the person needs to move on and not try to reconcile.

The gift of reconciliation leads to healing, both in the giving and in the receiving. It is a freely chosen gift. However, it is important to distinguish between what this gift is and what it is not. The guide can be very helpful with this aspect of the process. Since the guide is not a part of the experience or hurt or of the traveler's pain, he or she can help the traveler see what is true and what the feeling is. And then the guide can help with the healing process.

It is important to know what forgiveness is not. It is not forgetting; it is not denial; it is not ignoring the unhealed hurts and injustices; it is not condoning; it is not excusing; it is not condemning.

Forgiveness is one person's moral response to another's injustice.

It is important to realize that reconciliation is something different. Reconciliation is two parties coming together in mutual respect. The connection of the guide and traveler allow for the traveler to open up, let go, and work through the forgiveness process and then, if possible, work toward reconciliation.

Reflection on Forgiveness
by Peg Edera

It is a practice—every event that requires forgiveness requires a new journey with a new path. It doesn't happen quickly. It is a lifestyle, not an event. It is ongoing, and the path is not exactly like any other path. It is a process with an end product that one has to believe in, because one won't know all of the fruits of forgiveness until one actually tastes the fruits.

Some of the practices are:

Free Choice—No one else can make someone forgive another. One chooses to forgive (following a path that leads to some sort of fruit), or the person chooses to harbor the hurt, the anger, the resentment, the ill-feeling. On the road to forgiveness one may need to make the choice repeatedly.

Therapy—Often the effects of trauma are so wide and multifaceted that therapy is an extremely useful method for getting to the path of forgiveness. Many effects of trauma need anger and grief to be felt before one can begin the path of forgiveness. Therapy may be the most safe and effective place for this.

Spiritual Direction—The effects of trauma on the spirit are often under-recognized by the healing professions. Each person is adept at healing the psyche and the body and beginning to understand the need to address the healing of the soul. This is where a guide can walk with you. Often the relationship with God is also changed by trauma. Spiritual direction can assist the traveler in returning to a sense of something greater than the pain of this trauma.

Healing Practices—Studying and practicing physical and spiritual healing modalities can produce wonderful results on the path to forgiveness. Physical modalities might include yoga, tai chi, qi gong, acupuncture, massage, energy work, dance, walking, running, and so on. Spiritual modalities might include contemplative prayer, compassion practices such as tonglen and loving kindness meditations, visualizations, affirmations, gratitude practices, journaling, art, silent prayer or meditation, retreats, rituals, and so on.

Talk and Read—Take forgiveness on as a hobby. Ask a friend about his or her experiences. Speak about the path as you walk it. Ask a friend to be a companion on the path. Develop a reading list. Check out the Internet. Discover the wisdom of a variety of faith traditions.

Listen to oneself—Practice hearing and trusting yourself. You will know when you are ready to let go of the lock on the gate that is barring you from the path.

Quotations on Forgiveness

The weak can never forgive. Forgiveness is the attribute of the strong. ❧ Gandhi

Always forgive your enemies—nothing annoys them so much. ❧ Daranjo

The more you know yourself, the more you forgive yourself. ❧ Confucius

The remarkable thing is that we really love our neighbor as ourselves: we do unto others as we do unto ourselves. We hate others when we hate ourselves. We are tolerant toward others when we tolerate ourselves. We forgive others when we forgive ourselves. We are prone to sacrifice others when we are ready to sacrifice ourselves. ❧ Eric Hoffer

We must develop and maintain the capacity to forgive. He who is devoid of the power to forgive is devoid of the power to love. There is some good in the worst of us and some evil in the best of us. When we discover this, we are less prone to hate our enemies. ❧ Martin Luther King, Jr.

Forgiveness is a way of life, not an event. ❧ Judy Cannato

To "forgive" prematurely, before we have harvested the wisdom of our wounds, is like spraying cologne on garbage. ❧ Joan Borysenko

To forgive is to set a prisoner free and discover that the prisoner was you. ❧ Lewis B. Smedes

Forgiveness is the fragrance that the violet sheds on the heel that has crushed it. ❧ Mark Twain

In the end, forgiveness simply means never putting another person out of our heart. ❧ Jack Kornfield

To err is human, to forgive, divine. ❧ Alexander Pope

Holy Writings on Forgiveness and Reconciliation

All holy writings advocate an attitude of forgiveness and tolerance of others' mistakes, even when the other causes offense or injury. Forgiveness is more helpful than holding a grudge, which blocks the spirit.

Subvert anger by forgiveness. ❧ Jainism

The best deed of a great (person) is to forgive and forget. ❧ Islam

Where there is forgiveness, there is God Himself. ❧ Sikhism

If you efface and overlook and forgive, then lo! God is forgiving, merciful. ❧ Islam

The superior man tends to forgive wrongs and deals leniently with crimes. ❧ Confucianism

If you are offering your gift at the altar, and there remember that your brother has something against you, leave your gift there before the altar and go; first be reconciled to your brother, and then come and offer your gift. ❧ Christianity

The Day of Atonement atones for sins against God, not for sins against man, unless the injured person has been appeased. ❧ Judaism

Show endurance in humiliation and bear no grudge. ❧ Taoism

You shall not take vengeance or bear any grudge against the sons of your own people, but you shall love your neighbor as yourself: I am the Lord. ❧ Judaism and Christianity

Questions on Forgiveness

1. Which quotation on forgiveness most speaks to you?

2. Why is forgiveness for ourselves?

3. What is the value of holding resentment and anger in your heart?

4. How are forgiveness and letting go tied together?

5. What is the difference between forgiveness and reconciliation?

Response to Questions on Forgiveness

1. Which quotation on forgiveness most speaks to you?

The quotation about setting a prisoner free touches me. I am the one who holds on to the resentment and fear, giving the person a place in my heart. I need to remember that I am in charge of keeping my life free of hurt and pain.

2. Why is forgiveness for ourselves?

Because we are responsible for having a clean heart, and it is our responsibility to not give over our power to anyone, especially someone who has hurt us.

3. What is the value of holding resentment and anger in your heart?

Not sure there is any, but that doesn't mean I still do not hold on to it. It is so much a part of my life. I need to let it go.

4. How are forgiveness and letting go tied together?

Forgiveness is essential in going on the spiritual journey. If we do not forgive ourselves, or others, or both, we will be tied down to old patterns and messages. We will never be able to leave the past or begin to forgive. Forgiveness is the fuel for liberation.

5. What is the difference between forgiveness and reconciliation?

Forgiveness is something I do for myself because I am responsible for myself. Reconciliation is the work of both parties working to heal a relationship. It is always possible to forgive, but not always possible to reconcile.

Chapter Fifteen

Six Frameworks of Spirituality and Seven Stages of Spiritual Growth

Six Frameworks of Spirituality

Each person has her or his story, which becomes the beginning of the spiritual journey. The guides support the traveler on the journey by listening to where the traveler is. The following is a preview of the frameworks of spirituality, of where one might be on the spiritual journey.

Fall and Redemption—This framework is based on human nature and the need to be saved or redeemed. It is formed on the idea that a human being struggles to be good and is challenged by the world of greed, jealousy, envy; that a human being is conditioned away from his or her inherent goodness by misinformation, lack of information, lack of support, or the "isms" he or she lives with; or on the idea that a human being is seen or sees him- or herself as "less than," or a sinner, and therefore needs to be saved. The Divine then becomes the savior, the way to redemption or salvation.

Personal Spirituality—This framework is based on a one-to-one relationship. The relationship is between a person and a spiritual figure: Jesus and I, Muhammad and I, Buddha and I. The relationship is established, grows, and builds into a deep connection. The relationship grows through stories, study, prayer, and reflection on, with, and through the spiritual figure. The person asks how would Buddha, how would Jesus, how would Yahweh answer this question, or how would the spiritual figure handle a given situation or solve a dilemma.

The Divine Infused—This framework is based on an infusion of the Divine into a person. The person empties, surrenders, lets go of anything and everything so that she or he becomes an empty vessel, a blank slate, ego-free. The Divine comes from the outside into. The image is of a full jar of water pouring into an empty vase, Spirit-filled words completing a page, a figure filled to the brim with grace. This process is relational only in that the person does the emptying, the clearing, and the Divine does the filling. It comes from outside and is a one-way process.

The Divine Within—This framework requires a container, an opening oneself up to take in the Divine. The person makes him- or herself present, sets up the space to receive the Divine into the self. The Divine is always there; the traveler simply needs to show up. So the person hears, listens to the longings, the desire, the movement, the transcendental questions that unfold. This model is very relational between the individual and the Divine. It involves the person making the space, holding the container, setting the table, filling the pool, and the Divine coming into the space, resting in the container, sitting at the table, stirring the water.

God Among—This framework is based on a community connection. It is social, connected, interconnected, relational, dependent, and interdependent. When two or three are gathered together, the Divine is present. This model involves being present to self and others, engaging, sharing, noticing, connecting, and listening. One cannot be in relationship with the Divine without being connected to compassion, justice, and service.

Energy—This framework is based on energy. It involves no Divine figure or image. God is seen as a verb, not a person or an activity, such as father or creator. The model is one of "godding." It involves two coming together, being present to each other, sharing the story, doing the cosmic dance together. It is the coming together that creates energy. The coming together, being present, being human to human is called "godding."

Seven Stages of Spiritual Growth

On the spiritual journey, both the guide and the traveler move through various stages of spiritual growth. It is important to discern what each stage is asking of the person.

The general population moves to stage four and seems to be happy staying in that place. There is no judgment as to where a person is on the journey, but it is important to honor the place where the traveler begins. Each stage has its own particular focus, foundation, way of praying, and rituals that fit the stage.

Stage One—Stage one is the stage of myth, magic, mystery, and story. Children are very connected to this stage. It is where Santa Claus, the Easter Bunny, angels, fairies, picture books, bible stories, games, and legends play a big part. It is a stage of wonder and delight, a place to be without work, and a place where it is best to let the traveler enjoy the experience for as long as she or he believes or is fed by the mystery and story. Everything is seen as black or white, and that is fine in this stage. Everything is clear and simple. Prayers and ritual are about asking for or planning for the myth or mystery, like asking God for something or setting out cookies for Santa.

Stage Two—Stage two is a very personal stage, in which there is a connection between the traveler and someone or something holy. This stage is where one connects with Jesus, Mohammad, the Buddha teachings, or some holy wise man or woman. It is based on a very private and personal relationship. It has a "Jesus and I" spirituality. It is a very safe place to be; it does not involve another person and is not a part of a community. It is about developing a friendship with something new, pure, and holy. Right and wrong are defined by what the relationship says is right or wrong. What would Jesus do, or what would the Buddha teachings say? Prayers and rituals are very personal and secret, like diaries or letters.

Stage Three—Stage three is where the person longs to connect with others. Ritual, going to temple, church, or a *songa* becomes important. It is more than just connecting; it is about building a system of belief and learning about a given religion or way of thinking and living in the world. This model is often empowered by a belief in a person's unworthiness and a need to be made worthy by something from the outside. Formal ritual and root prayers are a part of this stage, along with practices of sacrifice and atonement.

Stage Four—Stage four is a commitment to a given way of believing based on dogma, doctrine, and values. It has its strength in community for ritual, prayer, service, social justice, and coffee and doughnuts. Each traveler finds a history, deep relationship, sense of belonging, and safety in this stage. Social action, liturgies, sacraments, celebrations, seasonal events, and rites of passage are part of this stage. Prayer and ritual is communal and follows a formula or set of practices determined by the community.

Stage Five—Stage five is about moving beyond the communal aspect and beginning to have questions, doubts, and disagreements with the tradition or teachings of the community. It is based on personal responsibility for one's beliefs and values and ways of living in the world. A traveler often stays in stage four because of his or her history or connections, or to better serve the larger community through social action. But the traveler stops buying into the spirituality based on myth, stories, personal relationship, or teaching from a given tradition or dogma. This stage often happens when a person experiences the God Within or the God Among. The traveler begins to see self as a container of the sacred, as existing within self rather than far away or in someone else's teaching or image of the holy. Prayer and ritual are very difficult in this stage, because they do not necessarily spiritually feed the traveler. In fact, the traveler is often complaining about the language or ritual not being inclusive or not feeding her or him.

Stage Six—Stage six is where the traveler stops complaining about what is not working and begins to discover new ways of praying, new practices, and new rituals that embrace the idea that he or she is holy, inherently good, and deeply connected to a God who has never left the person. The traveler no longer feels a need to be saved. This stage is about liberation toward a new way of relating, believing, and being. It involves a belief that each person is an original blessing. Prayers and ritual move with wherever the person is, and the traveler explores many new ways: centering prayer, meditation, journaling, labyrinth walks, and spiritual direction.

Stage Seven—Stage seven is where the traveler experiences the holy everywhere. This is the stage where the traveler experiences the divine presence in all he or she does, in all his or her living and being. Prayer life and rituals are less formal and often happen less, because one is no longer trying to contact or connect with the Divine through ritual or prayer. The person is already at one with the Divine or sacred. The great prayer at this stage is a prayer of gratitude; the ritual at this stage is one of celebration.

It is very important that the guide be aware of where the traveler is and what stage the traveler is in. The guide must honor where the traveler is and guide him or her, especially when the person is asking the questions that might lead to the next stage. The guide cannot move the traveler from one stage to another; it happens through the traveler's questions and discoveries. Also, the guide cannot speed up the process, nor can the traveler. It is essential to grow into the next stage at the traveler's own pace.

Chapter Sixteen

Connectedness to All and

To the Universe

The spiritual journey leads the traveler and the guide and strengthens connectedness with all living beings on the planet. The work of the traveler and guide model this connectedness. Every man and every woman is connected, based on humanity, to each other and to the universe. A human today has a view of the world that is moving, that is in process, and that person sees him- or herself as a key player in the process. Natural history and human history need not compete. They form a unity if the traveler accepts the connectedness, if he or she lives in the journey.

This process begins at conception and calls each person to respect his or her body, the bodies of others, and the gifts of the earth—honoring the inherent quality of dignity in each person. When one respects one's dignity and the dignity of all, when one develops one's talents, history, beliefs, heritage, and culture, the rich diversity becomes a gathering of gifts. This means a guide sees the uniqueness in each traveler as a rich gift. It means claiming one's power and making the decision to be fully human. This is the major role of the guide: honoring the dignity of the traveler whom the guide is working with and helping the traveler by listening to him or her explore all that he or she is—beliefs, culture, history, and life story.

The guide and traveler also respect the dignity of self and others by eliminating any form of oppression that denies the dignity of others. This means a commitment to self-healing and working to heal the effects of racism, sexism, homophobia, or any other form of oppression.

Through the connectedness and the integrity to humanity, the guide and traveler are called to be honest and courageous in standing up for self and others. The guide cannot let one joke, remark, put-down, inhuman gesture, or activity go by without taking a stand in favor of the human community.

The guide and traveler must also respect others by treating others with true love and compassion and holding out every human quality as being inherent in everyone. The guide supports the traveler in not settling for anything less than all he or she can be. The guide helps the traveler see the good in him- or herself and in others.

The traveler and guide see the earth and the universe as a gift and worthy of the best and gentlest care. No one can use the planet as an unconnected object. The planet continually shows the guide and traveler the interconnectedness and interdependency upon the world and the world's population. Each person has been gifted with great resources. So the traveler and guide work together to be great stewards of the water, the air, the land, and the universe.

Connectedness involves relationships. Relationships involve accepting one's inherent human qualities. Every traveler and guide possess all human qualities, but some of these have been covered by old hurts, fears, or coping methods. Connectedness means seeing all creation as a mutual, relational gift, atom to atom, molecule to molecule, organism to organism, land to plants, plants to animals, animals to other animals, human to human, and back to atoms, molecules, plants, fish, and all things.

Connectedness calls each person to act out of love, mutuality, and presence. This means each person can live life as he or she is dealing with life, rather than having to "get it together" before he or she can get on with life. It means living life *now*, in the *present*. It does not mean living in the past, or living in expectation of the future.

In summary, the nature and dignity of all humans creates a connection to all the cosmos in a loving, gracious way. This connectedness is the ultimate purpose of human existence. The traveler reclaims his or her worth and dignity. It is out of the essence of who he or she is that the traveler connects to his or her power. And, through that power, the traveler reaches out to a guide to ask for support on the journey to connectedness, to the connection to self, others, the world, the cosmos, and whatever is transcendental.

A human act is based on clear thinking, on making decisions, on free choice, on awareness; it is acting, thinking, deciding, and feeling based on inherent human nature. That is when the traveler and guide are truly connected.

The glory of humanity is expressed by women, men, and children making the decision to live life fully in the moment and connecting to every living and non-living thing in the universe.

Reflection on Connection
by Annie Doyle

To be connected is to be in relationship, to be part of something, to belong. We join book clubs, card groups, political parties, religions, golf clubs, and groups *ad nauseam* to be acknowledged, to share, and to form our identities. We long to have a place of safety to call our own. We look to define ourselves.

This morning, sitting before an eastern facing window, in the dark, carried steadily on planet earth towards the sun, watching the morning star as I ride beneath it, seeing shadows lighten into definition, the light expanding, I felt such awe and such joy broken by unfathomable sadness. Here I sit, part of creation, sharer in God's unimaginable energy and presence. I felt overwhelmed with a sense of participation, of presence, of connection. I thought of Doyle, my husband—how he would have exalted with me in this sight, in the conversation in my head. Feeling at once separate from him on a human, physical level, but one with him because both I and he belong in creation, to the creator, and even though Doyle is dead, he is still part of this glorious whole. We are still connected. I still belong.

Creation is not and has never been peaceful or static. Creation is volatile and changing, violent and nurturing, hateful and loving, magical and joyful. Creation fights for survival. Nature is not safe—every animal is in danger from something. I am connected.

I am part of God's energy—then I am part of the whole. Which part should I dislike, not love, be impatient with? Which part should I love? I am part of the whole—what I feel for creation—I feel for myself. I am connected.

It is light, but the sun is not yet visible. Like life. I see the effect of the creator—but not the creator. My sight is limited, but my knowledge of presence is secure. I am connected.

I am connected to those birthing and rebirthing. I am connected to those killing and harming. I am connected to those laughing and crying, sleeping and waking, rich and poor, believers and unbelievers, all those like and unlike. I am connected with humanity.

I can choose to honor the Creator God within me and all of creation. I can choose peace, love, tolerance, and unconditional love. I have to make that choice daily, sometimes by the minute. I can choose to believe, decide to act and feel part of this glorious and difficult world. I can choose Namaste. I can choose to belong. I am not alone. I am, never alone. I am Connected.

Quotations on Connectedness

Healing yourself is connected with healing others. ❧ Yoko Ono

The greatest healing therapy is friendship and love. ❧ Hubert H. Humphey

The reason it hurts so much to separate is because our souls are connected. Maybe they always have been and will be. Maybe we've lived a thousand lives before this one, and in each of them we've found each other. ❧ Unknown

What a different relationship begins to develop when you realize that God is head-over-heels in love with you. God is simply giddy about you. He just can't help loving you. And He loves you deeply, recklessly, and extravagantly just-as-you-are. ❧ David G. Benner

You ask "for what" God wants you. Isn't the primary answer that he wants YOU? ❧ C. S. Lewis

Questions on Connection

3. Which quotation on connection most speaks to you?

2. How do you see connection as part of your spiritual journey?

3. Are you most connected to self, others, your work in the world, the earth, or the universe?

Response to Questions on Connection

3. Which quotation on connection most speaks to you?

"The reason it hurts so much to separate is because our souls are connected. Maybe they always have been and will be. Maybe we've lived a thousand lives before this one, and in each of them we've found each other." This quotation most speaks to me because connection is the contradiction to isolation and separateness for me.

2. How do you see connection as part of your spiritual journey?

The work of being human is honoring our connection to everything. My spiritual journey has strengthened my connection to myself, to my relationships, to the world, to the earth, and to the cosmos.

3. Are you most connected to self, others, your work in the world, the earth, or the universe?

I have spent most of my life being connected to my world by dealing with justice in the world. But through my work as a traveler and guide I have broadened my connection to other people. And now I am working on being more connected to myself.

In Closing

Today there is so much being written and studied on the topic of spirituality. It is important for people to look at where they have come from on their spiritual journey and begin to explore where their heart is leading them.

The past is needed to see how the world began to connect to spirituality and religion, how people have been affected, how the world view has grown and changed, who challenged past models, and who offers hope for today and the future.

The new cosmology, a new sense of who the Divine and who Jesus is, the exploration of other spiritual traditions, the connection of the ancient ways to the present model, and the rich awareness of holiness give us a great springboard for exploring spirituality. The Divine's work is the expanding and evolving work of creation. The work of human beings is to embrace the role as partner in co-creating this evolving and expanding universe.

So we conclude the journey for the guide and traveler. Safety, presence, and listening are woven through the entire journey. Being human, reconnecting to our humanity through healing and forgiveness happen along the way. Connectedness and community are results of the work the guides and travelers do together.

So, whether you begin or continue…It is a wonderful place to be. Someone asked the Buddha teacher, "When does the journey end?" The teacher responded, "Are you still breathing?" The journey never ends; it is the going there, not the ending, that is what the journey is about. This is true for both the traveler and the guide.

So, remember, create a safe place that allows you to explore beyond right or wrong, beyond limits, beyond judgments, and free of past conditioning.

So, be present, experience the moment. Don't let the past push you from the present; don't let the future pull you from the present. Be present, experience the moment, embrace it, and be at one with it.

So, listen to your heart, soul, mind, and body. Listen to nature, the universe, to the cosmos, to the Divine, to others, and to yourself. Listen to the stories all around you.

So, what helps you on the journey is articulating where you are, where you have come from, and where your dreams are calling you. It is in your story and in the story of others (ancestors and the people in our lives today), in the cosmic story and in the sacred stories from different traditions.

So, in telling your story and in listening to stories from others, you reach the heart of the matter. This is where you discover the good news, joys and sorrows, light and darkness, and your own scripture.

So, once you have created a safe place, listened, and continued to be present, you bear witness to your story, to others, to the truth, to humanity, to the world, to the universe, and to the Divine.

So, discernment plays a big part in the journey. You must continually discern that you are bearing witness to the truth and not to the ego or misinformation. You continue to peel the onion, discern what is true, what is right relationship, what is certain, and what is uncertain. You begin to embrace the mystery, and it takes you to a place of depth. The journey reminds you that the more you travel, the more you don't know.

So, as you experience your story, bear witness, and discern, you reconnect to your core, your humanity, your authentic self. You get to be human—no more and no less.

So, as you connect, you begin to love in the full human mode. You experience a life of fullness and abundance. You make a choice to live life fully.

So, as you journey, both the traveler and the guide, you are going for life. And along the way, you see where you have been hurt, where you have been less than human, where you have hurt others and yourself. It is a great opportunity for forgiveness of self and others, allowing you to clean up old stuff and reclaim your heart, free of resentment and anger.

So, as the guide and traveler go on the journey, you do not do so in isolation. On the journey, you encounter people of every race, creed, language, economic status, and way of life. You hear their stories; you experience their journeys, their joys and sorrows. You recognize the rich diversity all around you and see it as gift.

So, in the end, the journey is about connection. As you explore the questions, live through the stirring and let the movements take place; you grow in wisdom and knowledge and mystery. The whole journey leads to connection to self, others, the world, the universe, the cosmos, and the Divine.

Reflections

by James Michael Whitty

Inner Yearning: The Pull of the Divine
James Michael Whitty, 2004

Pausing and reflecting for a moment in our harried lives, we may notice a striving within everything we do. We strive to obtain some thing or condition that will grant peace and happiness. Our striving is relentless, always seeking something beyond.

Underlying the striving is an insatiable yearning one cannot describe or comprehend. We feel it but do not know it. Our yearning compels a response, an action to lessen the tugging from within.

We employ various life strategies to quell this yearning, always externally focused. The chosen strategy becomes our life's primary motivator and organizing principle. While we may find moments of happiness and contentment, the results are always temporary and unsustainable. Inevitably, our striving to still the yearning—whether through things, persons, achievement, religious obedience, or public policies—ends in dissatisfaction.

We take our first step towards peace and bliss when we realize that no amount of striving in the external world can satisfy. Our true journey begins with our first insight that the source of our striving is actually a yearning from within.

I began to shift my approach to life following an extensive period of extraordinary pain and confusion. Finally, after years of reflection, I began to recognize my persistent yearning for what it is—a call for union with the divine. This call is for all beings to live in accord with our true natures, to know our individual limits but also to reach our highest potential. With this recognition, I began to look away from the external world to quench my spiritual thirst. I looked inside and began to follow an inner directive directly related to who I truly am.

When one acts in accord with an inner directive, the yearning quiets. Within this moment, we know our actions are in rhythm with who we truly are. The more we follow our inner directive, the more our yearning melts into bliss.

It is, naturally, not easy to consistently live in accord with one's inner directive. Shifting focus from the external to the internal is difficult. Shifting focus takes practice and vigilance. When we commit to the practice, however, our yearning works to perpetually pull us into alignment.

I asked myself, "How does one live with this unrelenting inner pull?" I discerned that the only way to some measure of peace is by acceptance of the nagging feeling of *something better*. We must rest with this acceptance because our view of reality is necessarily incomplete.

At this point in my life, I have managed to align myself just well enough to learn there actually is a *something better*. This *something better* is beyond the understanding of those seeking resolution externally. This *something better* is not a thing or a feeling. This *something better* is simple recognition of one's unity with everything in existence and the divine power of the universe. This *something better* is living in accord with this unity in harmony with one's true nature.

Once someone first recognizes unity, the person starts to live with unity in mind. This thought of unity begins to open every moment of existence.

To live in unity, one lives from within, according to an inner directive informed by one's true nature. One learns of one's true nature by being present to messages from within. These messages come in the form of feelings, reactions, body sensations, dreams, synchronicities, sudden clarity, or moments when one simply knows.

These messages from within do not serve the needs of the ego but rather spring from one's true nature. The messages may even be unpleasant, such as a call to hard work, training, or sacrifice, or even frightening, such as changing a life or facing an unlived life. One who recognizes unity must learn to surrender to the actions directed by these messages. The purposes of the messages are sometimes known but often are unknown. One must act upon the messages anyway. One must act moment by moment without concern for outcome.

When one follows the internal messages, acting in accord with an inner directive, surprising and delightful things happen. Perspective widens. Fear no longer motivates. Certainty of action becomes clear. Relationships flow easily. Ways around roadblocks present themselves unpredictably. Accomplishments arise, but we know the source of the accomplishments is something larger than our individual selves.

Still, the inner yearning persists until one's recognition of unity is complete. We see ourselves in everyone and everything. We recognize ourselves and our inner directive as indistinguishable.

Failure and Loss: Discovering the Capacity for Compassion
James Michael Whitty, 2005

To live as our essential self, we must find our natural connection to all people and all things. We find this connection when we find portions of ourselves heretofore hidden or unacknowledged. To learn about ourselves, we must examine the best attributes we hide and the worst flaws we deny. This is a difficult task. Our most treasured potential we tend to protect from the onslaught of the world. Our protective efforts may be so effective we forget our best parts or view the assumed flaws. Our worst potentials cannot be faced, so fallacies are created that do not exist.

At some point, we may recognize something in our lives is amiss and that it can be found by looking within. We may come to the stark truth—to find true peace and joy, we must learn all there is to know about ourselves, however arduous the effort.

When one sees one's denied side in its nakedness, one will also see the unacknowledged potential for action or inaction. We must look deeply into this potential, be it pleasant or unpleasant, positive or negative, heavenly or horrific. When we look deeply enough at our own potential for action or inaction, we will see how our potential directly corresponds to the behavior of others.

We may look at others disparagingly as we do things the other finds inappropriate or unhelpful or damaging to themselves or others. Their actions are judged actions, because we feel above them. We see from the lofty vantage point upon which they place themselves. They see this way because the other denies the potential for similar actions or inactions, perhaps not of the same magnitude, but leaning in that direction.

In truth, all the lowly actions and selfish attitudes of others are within our potential as human beings. We deny this potential because we see ourselves as good, living within an appropriately constructed outward identity. If unpleasant behaviors occasionally break through our normally pleasant demeanor, we associate these behaviors with being stressed or "not ourselves." We ignore our dark side because it is too painful to do otherwise. It is easier to see the dark side of others, separating ourselves from them.

The lowliest human potential is within every human. The sooner we acknowledge this potential in ourselves, the sooner we can look at the world with compassion. When we see our own potential for bad action, our own potential to disregard the needs of others, we will understand the dark behavior of others. This does not mean we approve this behavior. It means we no longer distance ourselves from others, looking upon them with disdain. Once we understand our own struggle with our denied side, we understand the difficulty others have managing the same struggle. We understand each person's struggle because we know it personally.

Sometimes our unacknowledged side is so denied and deeply buried that we can only acknowledge our dark potential after taking a dramatic fall from our lofty perch. Our behavior may cause loss of a job, a career, a friend, a love, a marriage, a good name, a credit rating, or our possessions. When our fall is far enough and hard enough, we may be shaken enough to learn there is no one to blame but ourselves. We begin to see our limitations and our dark side and can do nothing but own them. When we abandon our grandiose vision of ourselves, we can see ourselves anew with not only attributes but also the potential for flawed behavior.

After a dramatic fall or loss, our capacity for compassion for others grows. We are compassionate because we now see ourselves in the struggle of others. The person is no longer separate from us. The person makes mistakes, but these are mistakes that every human being has the potential to make.

Living through Our Spiritual Essence: Following the Inner Directive
James Michael Whitty, 2004

A time comes for many people when the voice of religious authority rings hollow. The doctrine of an external God judging us feels false. The comfort of religious teachings is replaced by feelings of loss and loneliness. These feelings prompt a nagging fear.

Questions arise, the most important questions we ever ask. We find ourselves alone, pleading to an unknown someone or something or some whatever "out there" for answers. We go along, as we must, trying to ignore our unsettledness but we cannot break free. We ponder the essential nature and purpose of our lives.

As we ponder, we seek bedrock upon which to build the foundation for new life. Time passes before we reach a point of understanding that all existence comes from oneness. This oneness was present before the Big Bang.

All beings are created of this oneness, not separate from it. All in existence is oneness differentiated into glorious beauty and diversity.

If everything is oneness, why do we not see and act in accordance with this oneness? Why do we not identify with everything as our true self? Why do we feel separate and alone? To find answers we must understand that we cannot perceive the reality of oneness while disconnected from living as our true selves, through our divine essence. Living our true nature is the bedrock we seek.

Beginning the search for true self is a desperately dark time for letting go of old perceptions and ways of acting. We feel this way because we resist letting go of the familiar. We flail about, kicking up chaotic waves on the surface of the deep pool that is our essential self. Only when we commit to transformation will we come to the point of letting go of our ego-generated life. The surface waters then calm, and we become passive, abandoning actions dictated by the ego. We rest peacefully in this placid place.

Our spiritual essence does not allow passivity for long. We notice ripples on the surface of our pool again, ripples generated from the depths. These ripples reveal a call for action—creative action—directed from within.

We ignore this call because we do not know how to take action except through the ego. The more we ignore the call, the greater the agitation within the pool. Finally, we take the plunge in search of our essence. Once in the depths, egoistic actions and mental conceptions are useless. We survive by following an inner directive informed by an inner knowing.

Inner knowing comes through the body and the heart. We must feel our way to creative action. Nothing outside ourselves can inform us of the direction we must take. This knowledge comes solely from within.

How does one follow feelings generated by our essential self? First we must notice from whence the feelings come. Do the feelings reveal ego involvement as do pride, satisfaction, gratification? Do the feelings expose resistance as do torment, anger, depression? Do the feelings have a spiritual nature as do peacefulness, delight, love? When they are spiritual, determine to what the feelings relate. They are pointing to one's essential self, the divine self. The feelings inform us of the actions we must take. Knowing the outcome of the actions is unnecessary. It is best to act without concern for outcome. Creative action inspired by our essential self is enough. It is our contribution to oneness.

Discoveries within the depths, if acted upon, bring direction, reassurance, and peace. Our feelings, however, are not the end goal of our lives. The essential nature and purpose of our lives is simply to follow our inner directives without resisting. One tarries not too long at one depth in the pool without hearing another call from an even greater depth. The pool has no bottom.

Turning Inward: Searching for the Spiritual
James Michael Whitty, 2005

"Where is the spiritual?" This question comes during intense yearning when we feel lonely, confused or lost. We feel separated from "the spiritual." We ache for the spiritual in our lives.

When we feel like this, something is awry. What is wrong we cannot quite identify. To find an answer, we look at the world with suspicion as if it has let us down. As we seek an external thing to blame, certainly we will find it.

If we look hard enough at our thinking, that something is wrong with the world, we may find an odd misperception. Can anything can ever be "separate" from the spiritual? After all, everything that exists comes from one source. If anything is spiritual, then everything is spiritual. If we have felt the spiritual even once, then the spiritual must be all around us all the time. Indeed, the only real perception is this, "Everything is holy."

Yet, it is true that we view many things, perhaps most, as non-spiritual. These "non-spiritual things" may include a television program, the television itself, a plastic cup, a dollar bill, concrete, a steel slab, material wealth, certain clothing or certain people. When we look at these "non-spiritual things," we may notice we do not feel connection with them. These things seem unrelated to our view of the nature of spirituality.

If we look at this perception deeper, we will come to recognize that nothing is non-spiritual but rather it is simply our regard for a thing that feels non-spiritual. When we see something as non-spiritual, we apply a self generated feeling that the thing is non-spiritual. It is this generated feeling of ill regard that causes us to feel separate when we are actually connected with all that exists. If we are willing to look within, we will find this generated feeling reveals our own condition rather than the condition of the thing we regard as non-spiritual.

During my years of dark struggle, I remember having difficulty regarding anything as spiritual. At my lowest moments, everything looked black and bleak. The world seemed to purposely thwart my progress toward the life I desired. I felt desperately lonely. My life felt unbearable.

During my lowest period, I knew that something had to change or I would not survive. This was when I began to look within for the source of my feelings. I began to re-examine my view of myself, other people, the world, and my place in the world. Through determined and relentless self examination, I uncovered erroneous view after erroneous view.

When we turn our suspicions inward, looking at ourselves as the source of our feelings, we begin to let go of external causes. As we untangle internal struggles, our view of life slowly changes. We start to see beauty where we saw ugliness. We start to feel love, hope, and compassion where we saw threat, gloom, and human failure. Indeed, the more we examine our perceptions of separateness, the more foolish they appear.

As we lift our veil of separateness, we unveil the spiritual. We see beauty in the rain and naked trees of winter. We find compassion for those striving for wealth, power or gain. We appreciate the ravaging behavior of nature. We identify with the accused. We understand the purpose of struggle and death.

When we turn inward, only one thing changes—our regard for everything. We find the spiritual everywhere.

Feelings of Separation: Opportunities for Spiritual Growth
James Michael Whitty, 2006

It is easy to notice the error ridden ways and foolishness of others. They do not think or act like we do. They live odd life styles. They have different life goals and worldviews. They have different values and morals. They contribute little to our favored world or perhaps even hurt that world. We fail to see commonality. We feel apart from them, maybe even opposed. Without them, nothing would be lost. So we may feel.

To live as a spiritual being, we must live as our true selves, recognizing and honoring our connectedness with all of life. To embrace our connectedness, we must learn to integrate the portion of reality we regard as "not me." We cannot live as our true selves if we view "the other" as unworthy of our love and caring. Our feelings of separation prevent us from fully identifying with the other.

Feelings of separation, once recognized and acknowledged, provide opportunities for spiritual growth. We grow spiritually by learning about ourselves. We learn about ourselves by examining how we regard "the other" in our lives. Our regard for others illuminates parts of ourselves that need attention. Our regard for others reflects our internal state of being.

During one troubled period in my life, I looked upon everyone with some degree of disdain. Everyone seemed to be part of a conspiracy to thwart me from living the life I wanted to live. No one cooperated. Gradually, I noticed that blaming others did not make things better but actually made things worse. Rather than looking at others for the source of my troubles, I began to look within. Through relentless self examination, I learned the only "conspirator" was I.

Self-examination is a challenging endeavor. It requires a close look at how we relate to everything in our lives. Through questioning our own attractions, reactions, motives, and worldviews, we come to understand ourselves. We find flaws and character defects hitherto unknown to us. We also find attributes and capacities we have hidden from ourselves. Finally, we recognize our common potential for positive and negative actions with all of humanity.

One self examination technique is to check in on your attitude towards others while in group settings. Direct your attention to each individual in the room, one by one, to see how you regard them. When you feel any hint of negativity towards someone, you have found something within to explore. There is some characteristic or behavior of the person that means something for you personally, something you need to comprehend and resolve. It can be surprising how your regard for the person improves once you have dealt with your own issue. Often your attitude towards the person converts to delight because you can now see the best in them. Your negativity no longer cloaks their value.

Another self-examination technique is to follow your behavior as you move about your day. Are you struggling with someone? Identify your role in the struggle. Are you feeling anxious? Probe why. Do you feel aggressive? Examine your motives. Do you feel avoidant, defensive or protective? Admit your fears. Have you reacted strongly to another's action? Check your life's balance. Do you worry? Find your attachments. The more you watch yourself, the more you will learn that "the other" is not separate or opposed to you but, rather, your spiritual teacher.

We are called to the highest spiritual realization. We are called to know our essence. By integrating the other, identifying with all existing, our feelings of separation dissolve completely. We discover our true nature.

Embracing Not Knowing: Accepting Life's Natural Flow
James Michael Whitty, April 2006

How disappointed we can be when our expectations fail to bear fruit. We want things to go a certain way, and we think and plan and work and hope. Sometimes our desires come to fruition but often they do not. Our motives can be selfish or pure, focused on our own needs or those of others or the greater good. It does not matter. Pure motives have nothing to do with outcome—often things still do not work out the way they "should."

When we create an expectation about "how things ought to be," we make a grandiose assumption that we have sufficient perspective to know how life should play out for all involved. We have changed our perspective on life many times (for example, baby to child to youth to adult to maturity) but always we believe we have the correct perspective and plan our lives around it. Why should we think we have completed our evolution and discovered the most valid perspective simply because we have advanced a few steps along our spiritual path? Surely, we can see the invalid assumptions of our past, but it is tougher to see the limitations of our present views.

While experience can be a great teacher, and we can recall personal growth throughout our lives, we may at moments feel the trace of a perspective beyond comprehension. This is the divine perspective, the ultimate view of the workings of existence. We may not know or understand the ultimate perspective but we experience it all around us. The ultimate perspective can be perceived in the natural flow of our world.

A flower breaking the earth immediately senses warmth and bends toward the sun. The flower's roots bore through the earth around rocks and clay to find moisture and nourishment. Working hard but finding the surest route to its needs, the flower lives within the natural flow of existence. The flower does not know this route at the outset but moves in symmetry with the greater wisdom. We are called to do the same.

As conscious beings, we may wonder how we can live without grasping the greatest perspective. The answer is simple though difficult to implement—we must trust guidance far greater than our own, an innate wisdom that flows through the immense complexity that is the universe, a wisdom that sustains all of existence. In learning to trust the natural flow, we must acknowledge we do not know why things happen the way they do. We must willingly contribute our insight, talents, and best efforts all while accepting that our contributions may not yield what we expect.

The natural flow that sustains the flower has cycles. Nature provides life and beauty everywhere but also death and ugliness. What we regard as "good" and "bad" are necessarily intertwined and inseparable. To have birth, there must be death. For death, there must be birth. The transition between the polarities is difficult, so we feel pain.

When uncertainty unsettles our life or work, we have an opportunity to work through the ultimate wisdom. If we pause and observe the situation without judgment, we will discern a trajectory for the natural flow. Our next step will become clear because it relates directly to our perception. Working within the natural flow, our work and our lives proceed more easily. Surprising and unexpected things happen, delightful things beyond our imagination.

There are times when I naively feel I know the entire pathway for how something should progress. Working diligently from what I regard as pure motive, my expectations are then dashed, and I feel disappointed. Pausing and reflecting amidst the chaos, I remind myself I do not know why things happen the way they do. I surrender to the natural flow, relaxing into acceptance of failure if that is the next event. When I accept that events cannot be controlled, often something not planned or anticipated comes along to move things along a smoother path. I find myself as surprised and delighted as a child at play.

We do not live life alone. We are not here to fend only for ourselves. We are a necessary part of and connected with the whole of existence. When we suspend our desire to know and accept our role within the whole, everything enlivens and intensifies. Life becomes vibrant. We find our true manner of being.

Spirit View Transitions: Trusting the Process of Spiritual Evolution
James Michael Whitty, 2006

Humans like to settle and rest on a strong foundation of beliefs. We seek to nestle in the safety and comfort of "knowing" how everything fits with everything else. We turn from the discomfort of the unknown by building a philosophy that defines the purpose of everything. Once formed, our chosen beliefs allow us to go about our daily business with self-assurance. Deep inside, however, we fear flaws in our thinking.

We ignore our feelings of doubt by covering them with activities and declarations of personal truth. We proselytize those with other views, push our policies, and attack outsiders, all to protect and defend the foundation built with our minds. Notwithstanding our apparent self-assurance, the potential for a crumbling foundation lingers threateningly underneath.

The world naturally resists our chosen philosophy—our spirit view. In time, we likely discover holes in our thinking. As doubt intensifies, we step up our activities or declarations, or both. We do this because we cannot bear the horror of admitting the deficiencies in our philosophy.

At some point, we can no longer ignore the crumbling of our foundation of beliefs. We admit the failure of our spirit view. This admission feels dreadful. We feel alone, adrift, without support. We find our mind confused, our mood depressed, and our body aching. To find safety, we may revisit a set of beliefs set aside at an earlier stage of life. Of course, we soon discover the futility of searching backwards.

Feelings of isolation are painful to bear. We tend to look outside ourselves for the correction, blaming situations, events or other people for our feelings. This does not work. No matter how much we attempt to correct the external world, our anguished feelings of loss remain. We must face our spirit view and enter the unknown.

When we accept our transition from one set of beliefs to another, we travel the path to greater understanding. This requires trusting the process of spiritual evolution. This undertaking is uncomfortable but natural to spiritual beings. In learning to trust, we find our way.

I have made many spirit view transitions. I have learned about my transitions by examining them as historical events. It is altogether different to examine a spirit view transition while embroiled in the process. Indeed, I am in transition now, but I know this process involves evolution of my spirit view. I blame no one or the world for my feelings. Most importantly, I trust that I will get to a place of greater spiritual understanding. I will not remain adrift forever. This trust forms my transitional foundation.

As we shift spirit views, our next foundation of beliefs, though better, may not end our spiritual growth. We may go through the process again and again, perhaps without end. This evolutionary process flows within our nature as spiritual beings.

Gains, Pains, Pleasures and Loss: Embracing Life's Full Experience
James Michael Whitty, 2007

In our western world, the daily challenge for most is no longer a struggle for existence but rather a never ending loop of protecting ourselves from hardship, pain or suffering; or, for those flush with material wealth, finding freedom from boredom. Turning away from unpleasantness, we avoid difficult people, situations, and conditions. Suffering fades into invisibility. To fill the void of leading shallow lives without life's rawness, we fill our calendars with activities, seek endless stimulation, and surround ourselves with luxuries.

Difficulty and unpleasantness are natural and unavoidable parts of life. As I grow older, I notice a feeling of loss as I see my wrinkles and graying, feel my body's pains, and find a less powerful spring in my step. I know the feeling of a job lost, a relationship abandoned, and my loving mother's death. I know there is more pain to come. If I live a long life, my future will be filled with ever greater impairment of my physical and mental faculties, and the sufferings of my friends and family, including many deaths.

How do we live life knowing that no matter what we do, we will face continual disappointment, suffering and loss? The first step is to understand the polarity of the light and dark sides of life. We encounter despair because we hope. We feel the sorrow of loss because we love. We experience disappointment because we know delight. To successfully avoid the negative is to forgo the positive. Such a life would be free of risk but listless and meaningless.

With the understanding that everything a person does in life involves accepting polarities and risk and is ready to embrace life's fullness. People who understand his or her nature as divine being is at the core of experiencing and knowing the whole of life. Each person is here simply to "be" amidst everything as it comes to us.

Being is anything but a passive activity. When faced with failure or loss, emotions naturally emerge. Some people want to deny and suppress them. We must understand, however, that these feelings—whether sorrow, rage or despair—are human feelings. In denying them, we deny our humanity. Other people wallow in their feelings or obsess over them. When lost in our feelings, we cannot understand them nor find a place for them in our being. Our spiritual growth thus stagnates.

Being means fully embracing our feelings, whether positive or negative. For full embrace, we must actively and consciously feel whatever emotions come to us. We must embrace the intensity of our feelings and know them fully. Only after a full, conscious embrace will our feelings subside to a manageable level and find their place within our being.

When experiencing a difficult event, I find private time to directly face my feelings. I take them head on with whatever emotive action comes—tears, moans, or bellows. I honor the moment, no matter how intense. I accept grieving as the necessary price of knowing life's positive side. Gradually and surely, the intensity softens, and I find a place for the event and my feelings about it within my being.

When we fully open up to our feelings, we find a richness of being flowing through us. Our lives gain meaning and we gather emotional strength. We may find desire to engage the world beyond ordinary day-to-day life. We may look for opportunities to care for others, all beings on this earth or the earth itself.

By embracing all sides of life, we are able to move beyond our individual selves to experience the richness of our greater common existence. We will hope when we encounter despair. We will love amidst the sorrow of loss. We will find delight in the face of disappointment. That is truly being.

Creativity: Living the Uncertainty
James Michael Whitty, 2007

Slouching pensively before the work of art, his heart beats furiously while his favored hand holds his throat. He adores the rendering like a new lover...exhilarated...inflamed...a plethora of possibilities. He hates this piece of art as well, for these very possibilities...and responsibilities...and an unlived life.

Oh, how we marvel at brilliant, creative expressions of others. We delight at breathtaking depictions, unexpected twists and truthful surprises. We honor those with talent, inspiration, and the courage to find new ways to say what is true, or find true ways to say what is new. Deep inside, we know our amazement comes from believing, "I can't do that. I am not creative." We suffer silently amidst our shame.

The mere contemplation of creating something from scratch stops us cold. We freeze with doubt. Our attempt to conjure up an idea yields nothing but blankness. If an idea manages to surface, we find ourselves terror stricken by the thought of attempting an expression of it. We turn to watch others or divert our attention to something else.

Humans are naturally creative beings. Yet, our creativity frightens us, and understandably so. To express our creative urges, we must enter the unknown, risk making mistakes, discipline ourselves to learning technique, find freedom within the discipline, accept rejection and failure and face the enormity of our unlimited potential.

Readily aware of our technical limitations, we think our creations must be perfect or we cannot begin. Maybe our idea involves a painting, and we have never touched a brush. Maybe we have a story to tell yet we struggle putting words on paper. Maybe an original song enters our head but we have never touched a musical instrument.

For decades, I was plagued with fear of my creative impulses. I gloried in the works of others (and still do). Artistic inspirations flowed but only within. Amidst an intense mid-life transition, I reached a state of desperation intense enough to overwhelm my fear of taking creative risks. Following a long hidden dream, I enrolled in an art class.

Holding a brush for the first time, I dipped it into paint and gently rubbed the canvas. *Nothing magical happened.* I felt tight and afraid, dumbstruck by the task of rendering. I had no idea what I was doing. My results were disappointing, my dream vanquished.

In my next class, I surrendered to the learning process and, surprisingly, I opened up. Something within connected with something greater, and my brush explored its own path on the canvas. I lost track of time. I felt an inner expansiveness beyond my ability to describe with words. I discovered I could actually make representations I sought to make, not always but often enough for delight. I had found my creative outlet.

Do I paint now? Yes, and I still struggle with doubt. I love painting and have a few satisfying results; but the better I get, the more I hesitate, delay or make myself too busy with the rest of my life. My spouse asks me when she returns home from the day's excursions, "Did you paint today?" Far too often I respond, "No, I was far too busy *not* painting." The canvas may always beckon but fear always persists.

Fear is the dark side of the creativity polarity. Every writer or painter struggles with the fear of not knowing whether—this time—their vision can be successfully completed. Will their technique be adequate for the new task chosen? Will this current effort be disappointing? Are they reaching far enough? Is their work true enough? Will the risk taken be demeaned or rewarded? Will their muse inspire another idea? This is the life of a creative person.

With the focused intensity and daring of a cliff diver, he smears the brush wet with paint across the bare canvas...committing...accepting...knowing he can always start anew. The mere gesture wells delight within. Brush lifted, he steps back to assess...A life now lived.

Future Moments: Looking Back in a Life
James Michael Whitty 2008

A moment to come that I wish for you:

A very old woman [or man], though her body moves slowly through this and that pain, a softness and strong confidence persists in her carriage as she reflects back on her life. She smiles sweetly and knowingly as she recalls her childhood and life, as her long gone parents pop forth in her memory with their support and delight in her every breath. Surely she achieved things in this world for them and herself. Surely she suffered life's slings and arrows as all do and found strength and endurance in her disappointments and losses. Surely she maintained a loving relationship with her family amidst all the complexities of a life lived in our chaotic world.

She sees her family before her—blood related and chosen—all generations being themselves and allowed to be just that. This matriarch wouldn't have it any other way. She knows life is meant for living, all of it with all sides of it exposed for the viewing. She knows nothing can hide forever, and she loves it all, even the hard stuff and the sad stuff, even the tragic.

She has come to see the worth in every being. She sees value everywhere, even in the evil ones who make the strongest attempts to cover anything good within them. She has explored within and observed in others that both sides exist within every being. She understands the challenge of life and knows everyone does his and her best though so many foul it up for lack of knowing how to do anything differently.

She feels satisfied she met her commitment to living a good life and forgives herself for her failings and mistakes. She remembers her loved ones with their best intentions having the same struggles. She forgives them for their fumblings, as well for those of others she has encountered.

Through the years she found a way to leave the prison of the past and live life freshly every day. Though she achieved all most could want in the external world and worked her way through difficulties, challenges and sorrow, after awhile all that became essentially meaningless as she found within herself the universal love binding the whole affair of existence.

She can let go now but it really does not matter to her. Every day for her is the pure gift it was when she was two years old. She smiles, "Let the days come, one at a time for as long as they do."

You can have it all, dear ones. Just remember that what you think of as "all" may not be. Life has a way of surprising you.

Through a Dark Night: Lost Amidst the Familiar
James Michael Whitty, April 2009

What I could see before I see no longer
Clarity has faded into obscurity
What had meaning before I regard as hollow
I feel utterly lost amidst the familiar

This describes how I felt upon entering the most intense period of my life. Up to that point, my life had direction and meaning. My strivings had purpose. True, I traveled a pathway I chose from options others had put before me but I could see where that path led. I knew the goal and objectives along the way. I surely experienced difficulty and disappointment, even some failings, but I knew the steps to take. Then one day, seemingly without warning, the known became unknown.

When the dark haze enveloped me, I lost my internal compass. Nothing felt the same as before. My existence felt barren, without purpose. Amidst the familiar markings of my life, I found myself on a new course, one through a dense dark fog that confounded any ability to get my bearings. I could no longer see where I was going or what to do with my life. There was only one certainty—I could not go back. The old way was gone.

Not uncommon in our age, many people find themselves in this condition. In religious and spiritual parlance, it is known as *a dark night*. Formerly regarded as an experience solely for the religious, a dark night now has significance for those living a primarily secular life. In a dark night, a person's familiar approach to life simply loses its meaning.

> **"In the middle of the road of my life,**
> **I awoke in a dark wood**
> **where the true way was wholly lost."**
>
> **Dante Alighieri, *Il Commedia***

An uncanny thing about a dark night—a person cannot perceive they have entered it. One knows things are not right but cannot recognize the special process underway. The path forward must be obscure or the person would not travel it. One within a dark night must reach the point when they are ready to abandon a deeply embedded approach to life in favor of a new approach, one heretofore unknown. It takes courage and endurance to commit to this journey.

By necessity a confusing and solitary journey, one must wander through a dark night without guideposts. Other people may be near—those who love you or regard you highly—but since they cannot fathom the nature and depth of your struggle, they cannot point the way. Only you can find your new meaning.

Frustration with the process for finding new meaning may result in depression, perhaps severe depression with its coping mechanisms. A dark night and depression, however, are not synonymous. In a dark night, a person retains effectiveness at work, compassion for others and a sense of humor. A depressed person loses access to these abilities. A person can get treatment for depression but must *experience* a dark night.

Not everyone makes it through a dark night. Some become rigid and bitter while others engage in self-destructive behavior. To avoid these outcomes and find a way to the dawn, a person must face a moment of surrender. With complete submission, one must surrender attachments to old goals, ways of thinking and approaches to life in favor of something new, something for which one only has an inkling.

I clearly remember my moment of surrender. Overwhelmed with frustration and hopelessness, in one journal entry I gave up goals, hopes, and desires I held since my youth. I committed to following some natural process, which I did not control, and a new purpose for which I had only the barest of understanding.

A dark night does not end with the moment of surrender. It takes a lot of soul searching and practice to alter one's habits and align them with the new purpose. With time, one fully embraces a fresh way to look at life and an ever-deepening love for *It All*.

Amidst Transitional Change: A Time for Action
James Michael Whitty, 2010

People in the throes of transitional change can reach the point of committing to fundamental alteration to their lives. Though difficult, abandoning an old view of life or way of living may be relatively easy once one reaches a point of surrender. Facing the question, *"What do I do next?"* can be much tougher. The unknowns concerning potential actions and new directions can leave a person either stymied or in a furious dither, hopping amongst various activities with no particular focus. Neither will blaze a pathway to a satisfactory new life.

I faced these condition years ago following my moment of surrender amidst a transitional crisis. After several months of retreat into intense internal discovery where I deliberately encountered some no longer avoidable truths about myself, I knew I had to re-engage the external world. I had largely abandoned my old approach to life and now looked for a new approach. I faced a disorienting blank slate, potentiality without definition. Wanting something familiar to lean upon, I found nothing (except my supportive spouse). Rife with fear I might add more mistakes to a lifetime's long list, I froze and took no action at all. Rather, I pondered new directions ad infinitum as if mere contemplation would yield obvious answers. I found myself stuck.

This *stuckness* can be apparent to those around the person confronting transitional change. Sometimes, the stuck person may be unaware, blaming their circumstance upon everyone but themselves. *No one understands; opportunities are unavailable; the world will not cooperate*, they may say. At other times, the stuck person may have an inkling of an attractive untried avenue or an intriguing pathway but thinks through the idea to the point of exhaustion trying to predict every outcome before taking the first steps.

Moving into change requires boldness, courage, and patience. Early on, ideas for action will come, and the seeker will dismiss them because of uncertainty. Requiring a complete plan or known outcomes tends to impede action.

Not all ideas for action are good ones. Some ideas will come from others or a desire for ego gratification rather than the soul. Confusion can fog the ability to differentiate the appropriateness for the seeker. Before long, analysis must end and some choices made. The advice of confidents can help but only the seeker can risk making decisions.

Until a seeker begins to realize the nature of her soul, she may have to rely upon a trial and error process to differentiate enriching courses of action from poor ones. A non-soul-based course of action requires *grind-it-out* effort.

Though such activities temporarily may provide ego gratification, over time the seeker feels drained and certainly not enriched by them. At some point, it becomes apparent to the seeker this line of action tends to subtract rather than add to life.

A course closely aligned with the seeker's nature will blossom and yield fruit, not necessarily immediately but through appropriate attention and effort. The seeker often experiences feelings of lightness and effortless focus while undertaking activities associated with an appropriate course of action. The tools used feel comfortable, even delightful. These activities may involve hard work and commitment but the seeker joyfully accepts these burdens.

When one seeks change of a comprehensive nature, actions may need to occur in several areas, whether with work, relationships, domestic, intellectual, creativity, spirituality or something else. Change in one area may not complete transition to a new life. Despite success in one area, unaddressed change in another area will emerge later for resolution.

Through experimentation, a seeker abandons some activities and continues development of others she finds enriching. Over time, the seeker learns the nature of her own soul and constructs a new life aligned with her essential nature.

Loneliness: A Call to Connection
James Michael Whitty, 2011

"I feel like I am on the dark side of the moon—cold, stark, and utterly alone."

I made this statement many years ago to describe an intense feeling of desolation. I had friends, coworkers, and dear loved ones all around me. Work and activities filled my days. Outwardly, I appeared engaged, yet within I felt desperately isolated.

One can feel lonely in many ways—lack of companionship, longing for familiarity, spiritual stagnation, loss of identity—but, at its core, loneliness means separation from elements essential to one's life. The intensity of the experience depends upon the degree of separation. A complete disconnection feels as though the essential element simply does not exist.

Sometimes, separation proceeds slowly, starting as a connection set aside but still within sight, then, drifting out of sight but still within memory, and finally, one forgets the connection ever existed. Other times, separation comes swiftly and dramatically by way of an event, a decision or an undeniable recognition.

Whatever its nature or process, the nagging need for connection persists. In our time, many cover this pain of loss with false life objectives, desires lacking substance or a clutter of activities and electronic devices. Others simply *expect too much* from the good parts of their lives, attempting to wring more from a relationship or a career unable to deliver all of what one seeks.

Early in mid-life, I entered a hopeless period where essential cornerstones of my life disappeared. I felt abandoned, directionless, and extraordinarily alone. To resolve my crisis, I felt the need to find the *one true friend* who could deeply understand me and direct me away from my turmoil. I could not find that person. I was looking in the wrong direction.

Peering into the abyss of my loneliness, I finally accepted no friend could grasp my condition nor help me out of it. I had to do it. *The one true friend I sought was I.*

I closed the gap with my true self through frank internal dialogue about whom I am—pluses and minuses—and making a decision to follow the internal whims, draws, and delights I had felt throughout my life but largely ignored. (For me this meant artwork, writing, and creative expressions.) Some did not appreciate my new direction but I could no longer let that stop me. My feeling of loneliness was a call from within for me to acknowledge my essential self and to live my natural life in full view.

The world has expectations for us whether from family, friends, coworkers, associates, clients, beneficiaries or society in general. To make life and society work we tend to accommodate these expectations. We do not want to disappoint. Giving of ourselves is positive ...unless, in the course of doing so, we abandon our essential selves. In doing good works, we must not ignore our essence, hide our true nature nor bury our essential needs.

Our essence calls us to know ourselves, live our necessary life and find the place to do so in the world. In this way, we will feel no separation from the essential elements of our lives.

Fr. James Galluzzo

James Galluzzo has been a spiritual director and guide for 25 years, working with individuals, teaching classes, and giving retreats. He is an artist, author, priest, teacher, administrator, diversity trainer, and spiritual director.

An ordained Catholic priest, Fr. Galluzzo is the author of: *The Spirituality of Mary Magdalene, Jesus as Liberator and the Gospel Values, Quotes and Reflection Questions for Journaling your Spiritual Journey, Spiritual Writing: Be the Author of Your Own Story,* and *Stop Whining, Choose Life.*

He founded Allies: People to People, an organization that teaches a way of living and thinking that honors human liberation based on the Gospel values, and that works to end oppression of any kind: sexism, racism, classism, ageism, adultism, and homophobia.

Fr. Galluzzo is the director of the non-profit organization, Diversity as Gift that works to honor all and teach about dignity from a spiritual perspective. He is also the director of the Urban Spirituality Center in Portland, Oregon.

He holds a BA degree from Gonzaga University, an MAT degree from Reed College, an Administrative Certificate from Lewis and Clark College, an MA degree in Theology from Catholic University of America, Mount Angel Seminary, and Portland State University.

Fr. Galluzzo leads workshops throughout the country on Conflict Resolution, Community Building, Diversity, Gospel Values, Spirituality, and Human Liberation.

$15 US

CPSIA information can be obtained at www.ICGtesting.com
Printed in the USA
BVOW05s0206060315

390618BV00007B/43/P

9 780615 629995